ACADEMIC FREEDOM AND THE SOCIAL RESPONSIBILITIES OF ACADEMICS IN TANZANIA

Edited by

Chachage Seithy L. Chachage

CODESRIA

Council for the Development of Social Social Sciences Research in Africa

ISBN: 978-2-86978-243-3

Typeset by Daouda Thiam
Cover image designed by Ibrahima Fofana
Printed by Imprimrie Saint-Paul, Dakar, Sénégal

Distributed in Africa by CODESRIA

Distributed elsewhere by
African Books Collective, Oxford, UK.
Website: www.africanbookscollective.com

The Council for the Development of Social Science Research in Africa (CODESRIA) is an independent organisation whose principal objectives are facilitating research, promoting research-based publishing and creating multiple forums geared towards the exchange of views and information among African researchers. It challenges the fragmentation of research through the creation of thematic research networks that cut across linguistic and regional boundaries.

CODESRIA publishes a quarterly journal, Africa Development, the longest standing Africa-based social science journal; Afrika Zamani, a journal of history; the African Sociological Review; African Journal of International Affairs (AJIA); Africa Review of Books; and the Journal of Higher Education in Africa. It copublishes the Africa Media Review and Identity, Culture and Politics: An Afro-Asian Dialogue. Research results and other activities of the institution are disseminated through 'Working Papers', 'Monograph Series', 'CODESRIA Book Series', and the CODESRIA Bulletin.

CODESRIA would like to express its gratitude to the Swedish International Development Cooperation Agency (SIDA/SAREC), the International Development Research Centre (IDRC), Ford Foundation, MacArthur Foundation, Carnegie Corporation, Norwegian Agency for Development Cooperation (NORAD), the Danish Agency for International Development (DANIDA), the French Ministry of Cooperation, the United Nations Development Programme (UNDP), the Netherlands Ministry of Foreign Affairs, Rockefeller Foundation, FINIDA, CIDA, IIEP/ADEA, OECD, OXFAM America, UNICEF and the Government of Senegal for supporting its research, training and publication programmes.

Contents

Appendices

Notes on Contributors

Chachage Seithy L. Chachage was a Professor of Sociology and Chairman of the University of Dar es Salaam Staff Association. He had published extensively on Sociology, and written many novels in Swahili language. Until his death on 9th July 2006, Professor Chachage was member of the Executive Committee of the Council for the Development of Social Science Research in Africa (CODESRIA), which he had served in several other capacities, including as Chair of its Scientific Committee.

Mwajabu Kachenje Possi is a Professor of Special Needs Education, specializing in Behavior Analysis. Her teaching area also covers Learning Disabilities, Mental Retardation, Mass Communication Research, Gender and the Media. She is currently the Director of the Institute of Journalism and Mass Communication, Univeristy of Dar es Salaam.

Amos Mhina is an Associate Professor in the Department of Political Science and Coodinator of the Philosophy Unit, University of Dar es Salaam.

Joe Kanywanyi is a Professor of Economic Law at the University of Dar es Salaam. He has also been a High Court judge, chair and member of many commissions including the Tanzania Law Reform Commission.

Geoffrey Mmari is a Professor Emeritus of Mathematics, University of Dar es Salaam and founding Vice Chancellor, Open University of Tanzania. He was formely Vice Chancellor, Sokoine University and Regional Adviser (Eastern Africa) to the President of the Commonwealth of Learning.

1

Introduction:
Academic Freedom and the Social
Responsibilities of Academics in Tanzania

Chachage Seithy L. Chachage

When the Dar es Salaam Declaration on Academic Freedom and Social Responsibility of Academics saw the light of day in the early 1990s, African higher education systems were in a serious, multidimensional and longstanding crisis. Hand-in-hand with the imbalances and troubles that shackled African economies, the crisis in academia was characterised by the collapse of infrastructures such as libraries, bookstores and laboratories, inadequate teaching personnel and poor staff development and motivation. Members of the academy, university management, state stakeholders and the community as a whole reacted in different ways to this situation, each of them trying to cope with the status quo but also seeking alternatives. Migration to "greener pastures" was seen as a way out of the crisis by many academics, but at the same time the worsening of material conditions among academics and students resulted in growing activism on campuses, with academics protesting against the falling salaries and deteriorating working conditions and students protesting against the "cost-sharing" measures introduced by university management on the advice of the Breton Woods institutions.

It was in this context of crisis that the questions of academic freedom and the responsibilities and autonomy of higher-learning institutions were raised in the Dar es Salaam Declaration. Questions around better living and working conditions, as well as questions related to the social responsibility of intellectuals and academicians, were daily concerns of the more advanced sectors of the academy, and the hardships of their economic and social conditions did not hinder intellectuals from recognising their responsibility to look much beyond the problems of their immediate environment and situation. It was a time 'ridden with crises but full of hope' (Dar es Salaam Declaration 1990).

The present situation is very similar to that of the early 1990s. Despite some differences, there is no doubt that in the face of the present challenges we are at a very similar juncture, especially as far as our responsibilities are concerned. The Dar es Salaam Declaration recognised not only that all members of the academic community have a responsibility to fulfil their academic functions and roles but also stated that 'all members of the academic community have a duty to contribute towards redressing historical and contemporary inequalities in our society based on differences of class, beliefs, gender, race, nationality, region and economic conditions' (Dar es Salaam Declaration 1990).

It is true that since the adoption of this document a lot of water has passed under the bridge, yet the state of academic freedom in Africa, and the future of African universities as sites of knowledge and social commitment, are still far from satisfactory. With this in mind UDASA, in cooperation with CODESRIA, organised a workshop in February 2005 to bring together the staff associations of some public and private universities in Tanzania in order to renew their commitment to the basic principles of the Dar es Salaam declaration and its sister document the Kampala Declaration on Intellectual Freedom and Social Responsibility, also from 1990, and to reinvigorate the social commitment of African intellectuals.

In the context of the privatisation and marketisation of higher learning being promoted by the World Bank and other forces of globalisation, intellectuals have a responsibility to produce "emancipatory" forms of knowledge and to make sure that this knowledge penetrates their societies and reaches especially the mass of the young generation. This means a fight within the campuses, because the World Bank models are now being incorporated by university administrations and management as if such "free market" models are the be-all-and-end-all for everybody everywhere. Universities were and remain a contested terrain, where social contestation is expected to take place. As noted by Mkandawire (1996), the academy is one among many sites of the struggle for democracy. Like other sites of social contestation the academy is traversed by contradictions of class, gender, ideology and other factors. Virtually every kind of contradiction that exists in our societies finds its expression within the academy as well (Sall 2000).

For all these reasons one of the outcomes of the 2005 workshop was an awareness among the new generation of academics of the complexity of the problems facing the education sector and knowledge production in general in

Africa. The papers included in the present volume reflect the healthiness and depth of the debates that took place in the workshop. Being aware of the present challenges facing academic freedom in Africa, participants thought it would be useful to first revisit the Dar es Salaam and Kampala declarations, bearing in mind that any discussion of the issues raised in these documents should contribute to take the debates a little bit further. The papers that underpinned the debates raised crucial questions ranging from the very concept of academic freedom and its relevance or significance today to the implications of privatisation and marketisation of higher education on the generation of knowledge and social transformation to the obligations of the state and communities in the provision of higher education to the role of basic research in knowledge production.

The first two contributions presented here stress the question of academic freedom. In 'Academic Freedom, Social Responsibility and the State of Academia in Tanzania: Glimpses of Nationalist Academics', Prof G. Mmari stresses the fact that it is always easy to articulate basic elements associated with academic freedom, namely the freedom of teachers to inquire into any subject that evokes their intellectual concern, but that it has not been easy to implement or sustain these elements. In this context the contribution of Prof J. K. Kanywanyi, 'Academic Freedom, the Autonomy of Institutions of Higher Education and the Social Responsibility of Academics', calls our attention to the necessity of bringing more practicality into the debate. Arguing that the two declarations did not present any practical programme for implementing the principles they enunciated, he maintains that revisiting these instruments only makes sense if one of the results of this debate is to make provisions that will address the practical dimensions of the issues.

Kanywanyi also shows how in discussing academic freedom in Tanzania one cannot avoid its relationship with the development of the East African higher-education system. He concludes that several serious threats to academic freedom still exist. One of them, he argues, is related to the new conditions created by the loans that have made it possible for providers other than the government to establish universities and other tertiary institutions. This expansion of possibilities brings with it the risk that 'ruthless purveyors of programmes of doubtful credibility' will find a sympathetic market.

Very often privatisation is seen as a panacea to the crises of higher education in Africa. The World Bank has managed to create the illusion that privatisation is something non-problematic that simply addresses deficits in the management of administrative and financial factors. As a result many stakeholders, including more than a few well-positioned officials, have failed to recognise how privatisation contributes to boosting social inequalities as well as presenting serious implications for the quality of teaching.

In the case of Tanzania one important principal of equity over the years has been equal access to higher education, regardless of family background or ethnic origin, for Tanzanians who have done well in their studies. In his insightful contribution Amos Mhina elucidates the advantages of this system and discusses the destructive implications of the privatisation and marketisation of higher education on social equity and the generation of knowledge in Tanzania. He stresses the importance of knowledge generation for the social transformation of the country, examines what sort of knowledge is now becoming dominant and asks the vital question ' whether [such knowledge] enhances the emancipation or dependency of Tanzania' . Mhina recognises the need for reform in higher education but argues that the reforms should have arisen from an analysis of the particularity of the Tanzanian situation and not from standardised reform packages.

Against this expectation, the university administration went ahead with the launching of the Institutional Transformation Programme 1993-2008 which, among other aims, was geared at creating awareness of institutional strengths and weaknesses, finding ways to reduce the costs of training students, agitating for a "flexible" University Act to improve the autonomy of institutions and improving the working conditions and environments for staff and students. With the implementation of this programme the university privatised and outsourced several functions and reduced the number of support staff. It increased to some extent the space for teaching and student accommodation and introduced new training programmes and new management units and also introduced programmes of excellence aiming at responding to job markets. However the process in general was aimed at the privatisation and marketisation of the university.

As I underscore in my contribution, 'The University as a Site of Knowledge: The Role of Basic Research', the University of Dar es Salaam has reached a stage where production of "marketable goods" is given priority over academic excellence, and academic excellence itself is defined in the narrow terms of policy makers as marketability of courses and of "outputs" (graduates). In the final analysis academic freedom under the present conditions belongs to those who control and own the means of production and dissemination of knowledge, not those who generate knowledge. "Commercialisation" of knowledge, with international financial institutions and donors playing a central role, has been the main feature of the development of higher education in Africa since the Dar es Salaam and Kampala declarations. The trend has been geared towards privatisation of educational processes, programmes and responsibilities while at the same time strengthening state control.

Popular, academic and political thinking in Tanzania and Africa generally has ceased to debate on emancipationist politics, that is, politics which would lead to the transformation of societies in order to reach a stage where no one's humanity is contested. It is only with the recognition that universities can neither function like government departments or like businesses that the central issues of knowledge production and basic research can be brought again to the fore. The debate reflected in this book will certainly not breach the gap by itself, but it is surely one step forward. In order to extend the debate to the whole society, one has to go beyond the conception of higher education as a commercial product which can be left to "free markets" to determine demand and supply. In this regard M. K. Possi in his contribution, 'The Obligation of the State and Communities in the Provision of Higher Education', is absolutely right to state that higher education should instead be considered a "social good" where both the state and members of the community have to share the responsibilities and accountability in providing education to our sons and daughters.

Possi's argument raises the more general question of the relationship between the state and the community on one hand and the universities on the other hand. This relationship has to be seen in a double sense. Whilst the state and members of the community have to be socially responsible and take control in providing higher education to citizens, the education provided has to be equally distributed and socially valid. For instance, it is important that research results are consumed by the community and used to solve problems rather than ending up on shelves as decorations, signs of achievement or evidence for promotions. These and other similar issues show that the higher education system in Africa has a long way to go but that our workshop has at least managed to throw light on some of these critical issues, in the expectation that the debate will continue and grow.

References

Dar es Salaam, 1990, 'Declaration on Academic Freedom and Social Responsibility of Academics', (http://www1.umn.edu/humanrts/africa/DARDOK.htm), 15 August, 2006.

Mkandawire, T., 1996, 'Economic Policy-Making and the Consolidation of Democratic Institutions in Africa" in K. Havnevik and B. van Arkadie, eds.. *Domination or Dialogue: Experiences and Prospects for African Development Co-operation*, Uppsala: NAI.

Sall, E., ed., 2000, *Women in Academia: Gender and Academic Freedom in Africa*, Dakar: CODESRIA.

2

Academic Freedom, Social Responsibility and the State of Academia in Tanzania: Glimpses of Nationalist Academics

G. Mmari

Introduction

The concept of academic freedom emerged from the more general struggle for freedom of thought and expression, basic rights of any free society. Without academic freedom, scholars cannot perform their vital role of seeking and spreading new knowledge. Scholars insist on having the freedom to represent the truth as they find it, even if this conflicts with popular belief. Creative research is impossible if its findings must be withheld or distorted to agree with established views. Thus, the chief importance of academic freedom is that society benefits from the knowledge discovered by scholars working in a free environment.

However, academic freedom is interpreted in diverse ways depending on the beholder. Instructors struggle for the right to teach, the freedom to conduct research and the freedom to write and debate without fear of being dismissed. Students demand the right to challenge their instructors' views without being penalised. Institutions have their own demands too, including the right to determine what is taught and what research is conducted on the campus. Teachers on the other hand want a larger share in selecting the contents of courses and greater freedom to engage in political and social activities.

Since the birth of universities in the 1100s and 1200s, scholars have wanted the freedom to pursue their studies. Originally, this freedom was sought because their work was subject to church control. Those who held views contrary to church doctrine were persecuted. Classical examples include Galileo, the astronomer and physicist, who was taken to task for teaching that the earth moves around the sun, contrary to orthodox beliefs at the time. By the 1800s, there was freedom to teach whatever and to undertake any research in Germany. In the United States of America, there were still threats from religious leaders who were intolerant of certain scientific views, as well as from those who held economic and political powers. This situation led to the dismissal of several university professors.

In the 1900s, there were still cases of lack of academic freedom. Shortly after World War II, in the United States, the fear of the spread of communism was so great that a committee was set up called the US House of Representatives Un-American Activities Committee that created fear on university campuses and led to the dismissal of many academics perceived to sympathise with socialist or communist ideas. In the 1960s, opposition to the Vietnam War led to protests against military research on university campuses. Some groups were also opposed to the teaching of "irrelevant" courses. Students challenged the right of academics to teach and do research, while both staff and students challenged universities' right to decide what should be taught and what research should be conducted.

In the twenty-first century, several threats to academic freedom continue to pose problems. They include threats posed by governments who see in academic freedom a source of challenge to their powers, threats posed by the general laws of society (underlining the fact that academic freedom is never unlimited), threats posed by specific crises such as wars, economic depression or political instability. The level of threat varies under different political regimes. Some are more supportive of the principles underlying academic freedom, while others are less so, as was the case in Nazi Germany. Threats also vary according to academic discipline. For example, some regimes will impose no limits on the natural sciences but will impose strict ones on the humanities and the social sciences, or vice versa. Finally, threats to academic freedom vary according to the esteem in which universities are held by the society.

Academic freedom is more secure in societies where universities enjoy high prestige and is insecure in societies where universities have not yet acquired sufficient prestige.

Academic Freedom in East Africa

Higher education at degree level is about five decades old in East Africa. Degree programmes were first introduced in the region at Makerere University in Uganda in 1949 through a special relationship with the University of London. The University College of East Africa, as Makerere was then known, addressed itself to the basic questions of academic freedom – what should be taught, how should it be taught, who should do the teaching and who should be taught. The first principal of the college, Sir Bernard de Bunsen, relates in his very readable recollections how difficult it was to convince certain policy makers that Makerere did not have to teach everything from the British University syllabuses (Bunsen 1995: 89). He also relates the constraints of staffing in a situation where people had no university experience.

There was prolonged debate at Makerere on what the degree structure should be – the very specialised 3-1-1 structure or the less specialised 3-2-2. Some of the defenders of the more specialised degree structure were native East Africans who believed that this structure was the best guarantee to recognition of the degree abroad. In 1952, students demonstrated at Makerere due to differences of opinion over what constituted a "university – level" menu (Ogot 2003: 56). They also demonstrated against the Van Riebeeck Day celebrations honouring the first Boer settler in South Africa. Since these were the days of Mau Mau in Kenya, white settlers in East Africa saw in this demonstration signs of black nationalism that would signal their downfall. Thus, from the earliest days of university education in East Africa, students saw the university campus as a place to exercise their political right of expression and protest. This in turn gave governments a reason to see the universities as potential threats to their control of the civil society.

The nascent nationalist feelings of the 1950s found expression in the 1960s when all the East African states gained their political independence. The University College of East Africa, the University College Nairobi and the University College of Dar es Salaam (born at the turn of the decade) were joined in 1963 to form the University of East Africa. Academic freedom in the University of East Africa was enshrined in Section 5 of the University of East Africa Act (1962), which empowered the university to determine who may teach, what may be taught and who may be admitted. However, it was not long before it became clear that it was the governments that really decided who could be admitted and, since there were three governments in this case, it was not long before serious differences surfaced. Some governments favoured the O-level route, while others, having invested so much in the Higher School Certificate (HSC) beginning in the late 1950s, insisted on the need for A levels.

Governments also decided what subjects students should study, as determined by quotas set by national manpower plans. A student who did not accept the conditions had one option and that was to leave. In other words, governments decided to which degree courses students would be directed. Justification for this stand was the need for maximum use of the limited space available for the good of the young nations. In the name of maximising intellectual quality, professional faculties were spread over the three constituent colleges of the university. Common faculties were open to students in the different constituent colleges; but for the professional ones, students had to move to either Dar es Salaam (Law), Nairobi (Commerce and Engineering) or Makerere (Medicine). Nationalist inclinations soon found expression in demands for the "East-Africanisation" of the top university management positions and demands for separate national universities. Already, what was taught and how it was taught raised eyebrows, as Tanzania chose its socialist path of development. It is on record that governments which did not subscribe to this approach expressed their disquiet through their employment policies with regard to graduates of the socialist-leaning University College.

Governments reacted to expressions of academic freedom in different ways. There was the 1966 incident in Dar es Salaam caused by a student demonstration against the National Service Act. Students were sent home in October 1966. Southall (1974) reports that the Vice Chancellor of the University was not consulted, while the University College Principal called the decision illegal. In Kenya, the showdown came in 1969 when the government refused to allow Oginga Odinga, who had recently crossed over to the opposition, to address students at the University College Nairobi. The immediate cause of the government action was a very strong letter addressed to its leaders demanding academic freedom to determine who would and could teach at the University. This was not an isolated case on the university campuses, illustrating the fact that governments of the day were determined to decide who should teach or even speak on campuses. It is said that, as in Dar es Salaam in 1966, the Vice Chancellor was again not consulted. The provisions in the university act were apparently good only on paper.

Eventually demands for separate national universities led to the establishment of three independent institutions – Makerere University, the University of Dar es Salaam and the University of Nairobi – which were carved out of the single University of East Africa on 1 July 1970. The three national universities saw the light of day at the dawn of a very hectic decade. Within only a few more years, the East African political community disintegrated in 1977, and each state developed its separate political ideology. Economic hard times however set in, and some of the development gains of the previous decades suffered.

The one-party regime in Tanzania found expression at the University of Dar es Salaam in terms of who was admitted to study. With the Musoma

Resolution of 1974, students not only had to clear their academic credentials, they also had to have good character as vouched for by community leaders where they lived. A few cases of extreme interpretation, demanding membership of the ruling party, surfaced and were handled in a manner that did justice to the applicant. Staff and students did express views on what was going on, especially the high-handed manner in which the villagisation exercise was implemented in different parts of the country. Maji-Maji, one of the campus organs, was used to express these dissatisfactions but was itself subject to repression. Meanwhile, cross-cutting issues were taught at the Institute of Development Studies, replacing an earlier programme on East African Society and Environment (EASE). The Social Sciences were clustered around themes perceived to represent the needs of the nation. Academic freedom crossed over to the expression of the rights of individuals as citizens, and many graduates of this period are now to be found in key policy-making positions. Meanwhile the economic environment led to constraints on teaching and research facilities. It will also be recalled that the Kagera War was fought during this decade, compounding the academic freedom debate as national survival became paramount.

The 1980s and 1990s were a time when events beyond the university gates – and beyond national boundaries – impacted more and more on what was going on in the universities. The end of the Cold War came swiftly after the fall of the Berlin Wall in 1989 and opened up a whole new era impacting academic freedom at university campuses. Demands for multi-partyism grew stronger, and universities were seen as participants, not catalysts, in these political changes. In Tanzania, Mwalimu Nyerere stepped down as President, ushering in a new era at university campuses, where the chancellor no longer had to be the head of state. Ironically, the first such chancellor was Mwalimu himself, who was appointed chancellor of the Sokoine University of Agriculture (SUA) as soon as he stepped down as president. This came in the wake of demands by the University of Dar es Salaam to review the act establishing the university. Some of these demands, originally formulated in 1982, have been implemented piecemeal since then.

In August 1982, the attempted coup by the Kenyan Air Force implicated students of the University of Nairobi. The state did not take this expression of "academic freedom" lightly, and several academic members of staff and students left for refuge elsewhere. Some of the students (who were not necessarily involved directly with the coup) were allowed to complete their studies at the University of Dar es Salaam. During the 1980s, Kenya introduced the 8-4-4 education system, thus parting company with the other East African states on the question of who could be admitted to university. Kenya was effectively saying that it would admit students immediately after O-levels, while Tanzania and Uganda retained A-levels as the standard requirement for admission. While governments have continued to ponder this scenario, universities have had to make their own decisions on who should be admitted.

The question of access to higher education became central in the 1990s, as the East African nations responded to rapidly increasing demand for higher education. In Tanzania, for example, the 1995 Act providing for a Higher Education Accreditation Council (HEAC) has made it possible for providers other than government to establish universities and university colleges. HEAC has provided guidelines and machinery to ensure that the institutions thus established qualify as genuine universities. The 1990s also saw the introduction of information and communication technology (ICT), whose full impact is yet to be realised. With the new technologies, ruthless purveyors of programmes of doubtful credibility have found a sympathetic market. Rapid expansion has also meant provision of higher education with limited resources – both human and material. Moonlighting by academic staff has increased to the extent of seriously affecting their efficiency and productivity at their university work places. In a sense moonlighting is a way of reducing brain drain to institutions outside the country, but the quality of university products is bound to suffer. The global situation demands that universities produce quality products. However this is only possible if we go back to the basics and allow universities the freedom to do their work.

References

Bunsen, Sir Bernard de, 1995, *Adventures in Education,* Kendal, Cumbria: Titus Wilson.

Ogot, B. A., 2003, *My Footsteps on the Sands of Time: An Autobiography*, Victoria, BC: Trafford

Southall, R., 1974, *Federalism and Higher Education in East Africa,* Nairobi: East Africa Publishing House.

3

Academic Freedom, the Autonomy of Institutions of Higher Education and the Social Responsibility of Academics

Josaphat L. Kanywanyi

Introduction

When I was first invited to present a paper on 'Academic Freedom, the Autonomy of Institutions of Higher Education and the Social Responsibility of Academics' for a workshop on Academic Freedom, Social Responsibility and the State of Academia,[1] the topic did not appear to pose much difficulty. However, upon later reflection, it increasingly became clear that this topic was heavily loaded, as it involves consideration of three sub-themes, each of which could constitute a topic on its own for a sizeable paper. My aim is to address the exhortation of the workshop organisers to review the commitment of the various associations to the basic principles of the two declarations,[2] and reinvigorate the social commitment of intellectuals. However, to avoid an inordinately lengthy rendition, this paper focuses on just one of the basic instruments in which the three sub-themes are to be found. Since the Dar es Salaam and Kampala declarations on academic freedom were made over a decade ago, some questions need to be posed relating to practice, both in terms of implementation of the principles laid down in the declarations and of what has been happening in the practical academic sphere since then. However, it is not necessary to examine both declarations, since, according to a reliable source, the 'Kampala Declaration' is closely modelled on the 'Dar es Salaam Declaration' (Shivji 1991a). I therefore refer only to the Dar es Salaam document in this paper, the declaration that most of my audience at the workshop were more familiar with.

In revisiting the Dar es Salaam declaration, I will attempt to see if there are provisions in it regarding a practical implementation mechanism, particularly for the prescriptive aspects of the declaration. If there are no such provisions, why is this the case? If there are such provisions, then the question is whether implementation measures have ever been taken and with what results. If no such measures have so far been taken, what should generally be done to remedy the situation? To facilitate a focused discussion of the three components of our complex topic, I will address each aspect in turn, prior to a generalized visualisation of the topic as a whole. However, as one can reach a holistic position only by starting from a holistic perspective, my discussion commences against a general view of the topic, considers its three main components and then concludes with a general view of the whole complex subject.

General Critique of the Dar es Salaam Declaration

The Dar es Salaam Declaration was adopted on 19 April 1990 by delegates of staff associations from six institutions of higher education in Tanzania.[3] In its preamble, the declaration made it clear that academic freedom, like other rights, needs to be constantly defended. It states: 'But rights are not simply given; they are won. And even when won, they cannot endure unless protected, nurtured and continuously defended against encroachment and curtailment' [The Dar es Salaam Declaration on Academic Freedom and Social Responsibility of Academics' (1990)]. The substantive provisions of the declaration are explicit on such themes as 'Education for Human Emancipation', 'Obligations of the State' and 'Rights and Obligations of Communities'. Moreover, in Parts II, III and IV of the declaration there are not only normative ('shall') provisions but most of them are expressly stipulated as 'Rights and Freedoms', 'Obligations of the State and Administration', 'Responsibility of Institutions', and 'Responsibility of Academics'.

One therefore expects to find statements in the declaration regarding how follow-up actions will be handled, by whom or by what organ of the signatory institutions. One expects to find a provision on how the signatory institutions will carry out their obligations under the declaration and with what consequences or expectations for compliance or non-compliance. However, the signatory institutions, assuming the delegates had the requisite mandate to commit the memberships of their respective constituencies, do not seem to have established any forum, secretariat or other form of leadership that one can point at with certainty in the declaration or any instrument referred to therein. Who or what organ is supposed to monitor compliance with the principles set out in the declaration or to mobilise action in the event of non-compliance? Did the draftspersons and signatory institutions regard such a basic issue as irrelevant, unimportant or unnecessary? If so, why? Ordinary common sense and common practice would seem to require some kind of compliance mechanism. However, although the declaration made many fine enunciations, it seems to have left them hanging in mid-air without any legs to stand on, any heads to carry them forward or any hands to guide them along the charted path.

One finds an interesting, though controversial, explanation for this apparently inexcusable omission in a 1991 article by Prof Issa G. Shivji, the only article I am aware of that seriously attempts to discuss the declaration from a jurisprudential viewpoint. Let us hear him in his own words before making any specific comments. In the course of contextualising the declaration in terms of its 'inspiration and style', Prof. Shivji observes:

> The Dar Declaration overturns the usual conceptualisation of human rights instruments/declarations which on the philosophical level proclaim universal values and see their realisation at the technical level of justiciability/enforcement machinery. In the Declaration universal values are embodied and seen to be realised in the process of particular historical and political struggles. The authority of the Declaration lies primarily in its potential to *legitimate* the struggle for academic freedom rather than influence the setting of legal standards in a justiciable instrument. The aim of the Dar Declaration is probably most appropriately illustrated by the ringing call of the Algiers Declaration:

> 'May all those who, throughout the world, are fighting the great battle, at times through armed struggle, for the freedom of all peoples, find in this Declaration the assurance of the legitimacy of their struggle.'

> ...In keeping with the nature and tenor of the document, the Declaration does not provide any sanction for a breach of an article'. The 'sanction' presumably would be the collective social censure exercised by the academic community as a whole. (Emphasis in the original, Shivji 1991a: 129-30.)

If the above-quoted excerpt captures well the spirit underlying the Dar es Salaam Declaration, then the glaring omission of implementation provisions was both deliberate and ideologically motivated. What was produced was an enunciation of principles, norms, rights and obligations for the general guidance and legitimisation of the member organisations and individual academics. As for sanctions, there was felt to be no need for these, beyond presuming that there would be so-called 'collective social censure' by the whole academic community. But surely even such highly 'democratic' censure would need some organisational initiator whose leadership legitimacy would need to be specifically stipulated. Otherwise – and this is how matters seem to stand under the present provisions of the declaration – everything has to be left to chance and good fortune.

As Prof Shivji points out, at the very beginning of the declaration it is stated that, following the formal launch of the declaration in July 1991, the next step was supposed to have been 'for the staff associations to pressurise the respective administrations at their institutions to accord the declaration formal recognition. Eventually, the Government itself will be approached to accord the declaration political acceptance' (Shivji 1991a: 128). However, one finds no clearly defined person(s) or organ(s) charged with these stated tasks. The staff associations are not required to 'pressurise' the administrations of their institutions, nor is there any responsibility placed on any person or organ to approach the government to press for political acceptance of the declaration. Yet, when the normative word 'shall' is used, as it is in this declaration, one has to wonder how such provisions are to be enforced. Since the declaration is self-executing, in the sense that it is meant to establish legitimatising principles, the 'shall' becomes a moral or political, not a legal, justiciable imperative.

The Need for Implementation Mechanisms

It is now evident that the Dar es Salaam Declaration has a serious gap that requires serious consideration, even if this gap was intended by its authors and signatories. It lacks general or specific implementation provisions or any practical implementation organs. That the practical dimensions of the declaration are to be viewed, if at all, not in terms of any prescribed implementing organs and their performance, but only how, in voluntarist fashion, the signatories have lived up tIo the declaration's principles, makes further analysis of the significance of the declaration largely speculative, if not futile. One of the advantages we would all have derived from having specific implementation provisions in the declaration would presumably have been systematic reporting on matters and issues of basic significance to the declaration and its stakeholders. Observances and derogations alike would indicate what has happened along the path traversed from the launching of the declaration to the present day. We would have been able to revisit the provisions with the help of documented practical instances. We would be able to learn from both past successes and failures in implementation and therefore plan for better approaches and more effective action in the future. Therefore, one of my recommendations would be to revisit the declaration with a view to making provisions that will address its practical shortcomings without unduly watering down the declaration's principles or diverting it from its areas of concern, focus and emphasis.

Article 52 of the Dar es Salaam declaration, which falls under 'Part V: Ratification and Accession', is the only provision in the document that envisages the establishment of any follow-up body. Article 52 states that 'any autonomous staff association or autonomous student organization of an institution of higher education in Tanzania may accede to this Declaration by depositing instruments of ratification with the body established in that behalf.'

This provision has no parallel elsewhere in the declaration, nor is there any substantive provision under which such a 'depository' body could be established. But at least by way of exception, one finds here a sense of 'implementation practicality', if one may put it that way.

At the same time I can see no reason, either in principle or in terms of practicality, why the original and subsequent signatory institutions could not constitute themselves into implementing and/or monitoring agencies of the declaration, with accountability obligations for the various matters stipulated in the document, on behalf of an apex coordinating body representing all of them. Such a body could be responsible, for instance, for overseeing or monitoring implementation, and for pushing for adoption of the declaration by the state. Meanwhile, the signatory institutions' staff associations and/or student organisations could be assigned respective institutional matters under the declaration.

For instance, the provisions of Chapter One: Education for Human Emancipation and Chapter Three: Rights and Obligations of Communication (both under Part I: Basic Principles) and Chapter Four: Obligations of the State and Administration (Part II: Academic Freedom) could be shared between the two levels, each concerning itself with aspects that relate to its area of focus. The rest of the provisions – Chapter One: Rights and Freedoms, Chapter Two: Autonomous Academic Organisations, Chapter Three: Security of Tenure (all under Part II Academic Freedom), all those in Part III: Autonomy of Institutions of Higher Education and those in Chapter One: Responsibility of Institutions and Chapter Two: Responsibility of Academics in Part IV: Social Responsibility – would seem to fall squarely within the areas of the respective staff associations and/or student organisations. It would be necessary to have some common guidelines or criteria on which follow-up, implementation or monitoring activities would be based in order to facilitate consistency in reporting, dissemination and analysis, decision making and implementation, etc.

Academic Freedom

Against this background, I do not intend to say much about the sub-theme of academic freedom, since there is a danger of stating the obvious. However, some critical remarks need to be made on some of the provisions with a view to rendering them less ambiguous in a future revised version of the declaration.

Academic freedom is covered under Part II of the declaration. It is conceived of quite rightly as involving the basic rights and freedoms of members of the academic community (both staff and students) at higher education institutions, partly in their roles as members of society and partly as persons specifically engaged in academic activity as teachers, researchers, administrators/workers and students. As such the document draws its inspiration from international and regional instruments on rights and freedoms, particularly those subscribed to or ratified by Tanzania. The declaration also cites the post-1984 inclusion of a Bill of Rights in Tanzania constitution, noting in the preamble the Bill of Rights' provisions on 'the right to education and the right to opinion and expression which include academic freedom'. Therefore, it is evident that the declaration takes a bold step by relating the universal rights and freedoms, and the principles underlying them, to the specific interests and concerns of the members of the academic community in higher education institutions.

This is important because it means the declaration is not claiming anything special for any elite interest but only restating and reasserting, for the academic community, the rights and freedoms already guaranteed in theory for all. For that reason, in a formal sense, the declaration has complete legitimacy; it is an expression of people endeavouring to exercise some of their most basic rights and freedoms, namely, the rights of association and freedom of expression. This should augur well for the acceptability of the declaration to the state and the institutional administrations, whatever their suspicions about the import and potential implications of adopting or accepting it wholly or partly. The promotion of the declaration should only face the usual opposition from the conservative inhibitions and attitudes of institutional cultures, rather than any accusation that it is impertinent or even 'revolutionary'. Ironically, the difficulty of 'selling' the declaration to the powers-that-be may lie precisely in its unquestionable legitimacy. Its expression of rights and obligations in such lucid language is likely to pose an embarrassment to the authorities, given their frequent non-observance of these rights and obligations in daily practice.

In brief, the rights and freedoms clauses of the declaration are simply asserting, for all members of the academic community in their various lines of activity, the right to pursue the same rights and freedoms stated in the constitution freely and without unjustifiable interference from authority. To be justifiable any such interference must stem from clear grounds of public health, morality or evident national security, etc., and must observe basic democratic principles. The declaration also espouses the right of participation in organs of institutional governance by students and staff, as well as the right of students to challenge or differ with their instructors in academic matters without suffering any reprisals or prejudice in consequence. None of the articles states anything new or strange, let alone unacceptable, in principle, in a democracy. But what is of crucial importance, of course, is the actual realisation of the stated rights and freedoms, which cannot be accomplished without both pro-active and reactive measures being taken to assert, protect, nurture and continuously defend them against encroachment and curtailment.

The articles under Chapter One of Part II are generally well-formulated. They are reasonably balanced, enunciating individual rights and freedoms amply, but without prejudice to the rights of others or to generally accepted norms and principles as well as democratic culture. This is reassuring and makes the articles capable of standing up to generally accepted democratic standards and to the test of time. The exception is Article 25, which concerns among others, 'the right of students on academic grounds to challenge or differ from their instructors in academic matters without fear of reprisal or victimization.' To whom is this last phrase addressed? This right can only be exercised where there is a conducive teaching and learning environment which, among other things, includes a tolerant attitude on the part of instructors and an academic culture that espouses free and critical exchange of ideas. In such an environment constructive ideas, questions and criticisms, even dissent, are respected and tolerated. In such an environment fear of 'reprisals' or 'victimisation' would have no basis and would not arise. If there are grounds for fear, then students will be discouraged from expressing themselves.

Article 24, therefore, rather than requiring institutions to create, nurture and sustain such an environment, is pronouncing a right to have no fear of reprisal or victimisation, even in institutions where the academic culture is in diametric opposition to freedom of expression. What is important in this article is the pronounced right; the 'fear' aspect could be expressed in a separate article dealing with the obligation of institutions to create and nurture an academic culture and environment that espouses tolerance of differing views, etc. and that therefore removes any grounds for fear of reprisals or victimization by students or staff who challenge or differ from instructors in academic matters. If I may venture a suggestion for reformulation, the word 'fear' should be deleted and the whole phrase from there to the end of the article be rendered as 'without being subjected to any reprisal or victimisation or any other form of direct or indirect prejudice'.

Autonomous Academic Organizations

The provisions of the declaration on autonomous academic organisations are contained in two articles (26 and 27) in Chapter Two of Part II. These articles basically restate rights and freedom of association, assembly and expression with specific reference to members of the academic community in their pursuit of furthering their 'academic and professional interests'.

It is important to underscore the point that the declaration does not deal with rights and freedoms outside the academic domain. If it were to address itself to rights and freedoms in any other domain, then one would say it would be wholly or partly *ultra vires*, as it were, and would lack basic legitimacy. The right to self-expression envisages 'the right to write, print and publish their own newspapers or any other form of media including wall literature, posters and pamphlets' (Article 27). Being aware that such a right may be abused, to the prejudice of others, both within and outside the academic community, the article quite responsibly imposes a condition upon the exercise of the right. It is worth reproducing this carefully phrased condition in full: 'The exercise of this right shall have due regard to the obligation of the members of the academic community not to interfere with the right of others to privacy and in any manner or form that unreasonably arouse religious, ethnic, national or gender hatred' (Article 27). Anyone who is aware of the ugly incidents caused by the so-called Mzee Punch wall literature in the 1970s and early 1980s at the University of Dar es Salaam (Peter and Mvungi 1986) will easily appreciate the point of this limitation.

Security of Tenure

The Dar es Salaam Declaration deals with the issue of security of tenure in Chapter Three, Part II. Security of tenure is perceived in terms of entitlement to a fair and reasonable remuneration commensurate with one's social and academic responsibilities, secure tenure for those confirmed in employment, whose dismissal or removal from employment should abide by the principles of due process, and the right to know of any alleged adverse information obtained by officials in their course of duty. The general idea is that members of the academic community should be reasonably secure to carry on their academic pursuits freely and with a sense of tranquillity of mind and career certainty.

However, one wonders whether some of the expectations are not pitched a bit too high and others somewhat too low. For instance, Article 28 talks of 'fair and reasonable remuneration', but such remuneration may not amount even to a living wage for some, if not all, members of the academic community. The article also limits itself to those who are in active employment and ignores the issue of retirement. Security of tenure which does not look into the future after tenure ends is likely to be half-baked, if not fundamentally flawed. That is why the issue of adequacy, not just fairness, of remuneration is crucial. If one's remuneration is inadequate, the retirement benefits will be doubly inadequate! That is why members of the community will, before they come to that limbo, look for greener pastures elsewhere, engage in moonlighting sidelines, and thus fail to render the benefits or attain the objectives which the provisions enunciate to be the underlying considerations.[4] On the other hand, we should not forget that members of the academic community will, individually or collectively, commit themselves contractually to do or not to do certain tasks according to certain requirements, and that failure to meet these commitments may result in dismissal or transfer/recategorisation. Security of tenure therefore has to be understood as a somewhat elusive goal for academics: publish or perish, remember.

Obligations of the State and the Administration

The obligations of the state and the administration are covered in Chapter Four, Part II. In assigning obligations to the state and to the administrations of institutions, the declaration seems to assume either that these authorities will be convinced by the generally accepted nature of the rights and freedoms being asserted to recognise and abide by them or that some pressure will be exerted (by whom or what is not clear) to persuade them to do so. Since, as we have seen, no implementation mechanisms are mentioned in the declaration, the achievability, of the provisions is not envisaged by the document itself. In this respect, one obligation placed on the administration deserves special mention. Article 37 states that the administration has 'an obligation not to divulge any information regarding members of the academic community which may be used to their detriment in any criminal, or other investigation or proceedings of the like nature'. But surely if one is suspected to have committed a crime against one's employer or a fellow member of the academic community, or is threatening the peace and tranquillity of the community, it would be very strange to expect the administration to be willing or to appear to condone such conduct by refusing to reveal pertinent information.

Autonomy of Institutions of Higher Education and The Social Responsibility of Academics

In this section, I examine the remaining two sub-themes: autonomy of institutions of higher education and the social responsibility of academics. I do not intend to go into much detail but only to raise some issues for discussion.

Autonomy of Institutions

In Articles 38–40, the declaration spells out its view of the autonomy that higher education institutions should have. Most such institutions are of course established under individual statutory instruments which declare them to be 'bodies corporate', capable of suing and being sued, with perpetual succession and a common seal, etc. As such they may own, dispose of and generally deal in property, movable and immovable, etc. The declaration, however, is not much concerned with such matters. Its focus is on the independence of higher education institutions from state or other institutional interference, especially in relation to teaching, research and general administration. The declaration requires the observance of democratic principles of participatory governance involving all stakeholders. In particular it denounces any entry into the premises of higher education institutions by 'armed personnel, military or paramilitary forces, intelligence and security personnel or forces of law and order, singly or collectively', except under stated conditions where 'the Head of the institutions concerned has invited such intervention in writing; Provided that such invitation shall not be extended without consultation with and approval of a special standing committee of elected representatives of the academic community instituted in that behalf' (Article 40). These principles are laudable, but they face obvious problems arising from the fact that most higher education institutions in Africa rely on direct state funding, as well as funding by donor agencies. This tends to attract interference from those that 'pay the piper' as a matter of course, as it was.

According to a Commonwealth study conducted in the 1990s, the following were identified as the main potential areas of friction between universities and governments in developing countries:

- Who may teach and what may be taught.
- Who makes key appointments.
- Determination of enrolment growth rates.
- Financial and other resource management.
- Use of state security on campuses.
- Management of staff promotions and travel.

- Freedom to criticize the state.

  (Richardson and Fielden 1997: 30)

To minimise such conflicts, the study called for the establishment of objective criteria for funding and suggested that the function of setting institutional budgets and disbursing funds be given to an independent regulatory authority. This is already the practice in some Commonwealth countries outside Africa, and I would urge that similar measures be adopted in Africa, where state interference is a real threat to academic freedom and institutional autonomy.

Social Responsibility of Academics

Issues concerning the social responsibility of academics are covered in Part IV, Chapter Two of the declaration (Articles 46–50).5 These provisions are exhortative; indeed, the normative word 'shall' is used sparingly, as though it would offend even the authors and promoters of the declaration. Members are exhorted to accept a responsibility or obligation to do one noble thing or another! These do's and don'ts include fulfilment of 'academic roles with competence, integrity and to the best of [one's] ability and performance of academic functions in accordance with ethical and highest scientific standards' (Article 46). However no model of such 'ethical and highest scientific standards' nor any mechanism for the establishment of one is provided for in the declaration.

Members of the academic community are said to have an obligation to inculcate the spirit of tolerance of differing views (Article 48) and to exercise their rights responsibly without prejudicing the rights of others (Article 47). They are urged not to participate in or be a party to anti-people actions or endeavours, including those that may be prejudicial to the members of the academic community. They are urged not to compromise scientific, ethical and professional principles and standards (Article 49) and to contribute to the cause of redressing historical and contemporary inequalities in our society (Article 50). The provisions sound fine in principle but are very weak in expression. The militancy one senses when others are being addressed in favour of the academic community becomes musing in the direction of the proponent interests. But the more serious problem, the bane of the declaration as a whole, is that even here no self-regulation machinery or guidance instruments are provided, nor is the need for any mentioned at all. The whole matter is left to the good sense of members of the academic community to handle in the best way possible. Thus we end where we began after all, with no legs to stand on, no heads or shoulders to bear the weight of the task and no hands to handle it!

Conclusion

I have addressed a complex issue under three sub-themes, each of which deserves separate treatment. The aim of this discussion has been to arouse interest around and stimulate discussion concerning the provisions of the Dar es Salaam, Declaration. Professor Shivji suggests that the declaration 'will have served its purpose if it generates an African debate on academic freedom and social responsibility of intellectuals generally, and [on] the use of a legal format in crystallising democratic political perspectives in particular' (Shivji 1991a: 134), but if that is all that is realised from the declaration is this really sufficient for the achievement of the provisions of the declaration? Do we not need to do much more? Hitherto, what African debate on the issues raised by the declaration have we had? The very fact that the events mentioned on page one of his article 'overshadowed the document' suggests that something more concrete and more mundane was, and, is necessary. Otherwise, we shall have to wait indefinitely for another workshop to 'debate'.

Notes

1. CODESRIA-University of Dar es Salaam Academic Staff Assembly (UDASA) Forum held at Whitesands Hotel, Dar es Salaam, Tanzania, 10–11 February 2005.
2. 'The Dar es Salaam Declaration on Academic Freedom and Social Responsibility of Academics' (1990) and 'The Kampala Declaration on Academic Freedom and Social Responsibility of Intellectuals' (1991).
3. The Ardhi Institute (now the University College of Lands and Architectural Studies, UCLAS), the Co-operative College, Moshi, the Institute of Development Management, Mzumbe (now the University of Mzumbe), the Institute of Finance Management, Sokoine University of Agriculture and the University of Dar es Salaam.
4. For instance, Article 28 envisages members discharging 'their roles with human dignity, integrity and independence'.
5. Chapter One covers 'Responsibility of Institutions' in Articles 41-45.

References

Richardson, G. and Fielden, J., 1997, *Measuring the Grip of the State: The Relationship Between Governments and Universities in Selected Commonwealth Countries*, London: CHEMS.

Peter, C. and Mvungi, S., 1986, 'The State and Student Struggles' in I. G. Shivji (ed.), *The State and the Working People in Tanzania*, Dakar: CODESRIA.

Shivji, I. G., 1991a, 'The Jurisprudence of the Dar es Salaam Declaration on Academic Freedom', *Journal of African Law*, Vol. 35, No.1-2, p. 128-141.

Shivji, I. G., 1991b, 'State and Constitutionalism: A New Democratic Perspective', in I. G. Shivji, ed., *State and Constitutionalism: An African Debate on Democracy*, Harare: SAPES Trust, pp. 27-54.

4

Implications of Privatisation and Marketisation of Higher Education for the Generation of Knowledge and Social Transformation

Amos Mhina

Introduction

The debate on privatisation is usually influenced by existing crises. Privatisation is usually prescribed as a non-problematic solution to an untenable situation. In such circumstances, any opposition to privatisation is portrayed as support for a system which has failed. In Tanzania and elsewhere in Africa, the World Bank documented in the early 1990s what it considered to be a higher education system in crisis (World Bank 1994). When cost-sharing w as introduced and critiques of the World Bank policy argued that the eventual aim was the elimination of public education, they were dismissed as reactionary scaremongers, but now we are in a situation well beyond cost-sharing. Full tuition and upkeep at the University for "sponsored" students is payable on credit, and credit enforcers will be in wait when the students graduate.

Thus, it is important when discussing privatisation to recognise the weaknesses of the system that existed before, but then critically evaluate the prescribed privatisation and its hidden agenda. The marketisation of higher education includes closer cooperation between the university and the clientele, which increasingly will be the private sector. It also includes a new emphasis on income-generating activities such as short-term courses, contract research for industry and consultancy services. These aspects of marketisation are worthwhile as long as the intention is not to use them to reduce budget allocations from government. Some of these activities have been able to provide better financial incentives for staff in the light of the small salaries paid to them and have also provided hardware and consumables for many overstretched university departments. However there are indications that the government intends these activities not to supplement its own contribution to higher education costs but to replace them. Moreover, at the University of Dar es Salaam, there are indications of increased control of such activities by the centre. Finally, the marketisation of higher education has other implications for the quality of teaching and for the encroachment of a pervasive ideology of the preeminence of market relations.

In this context, the generation of knowledge for social transformation becomes an important issue. We need to examine what sort of knowledge is dominant and ask whether it enhances or the emancipation of Tanzania or increases its dependency. It is the social responsibility of our institutions to do so. This is highlighted in the Dar es Salaam Declaration, where it is stated that all institutions of higher education should strive to prevent scientific, technological and other forms of dependence However, we can see that the agenda for research as well as the general development lexology are set else-where and that our academicians and other intellectuals are engaged in activi-ties guided by such knowledge. One such concept is "poverty alleviation". Important brains in the country are pursuing poverty alleviation, but each new study shows that poverty is not budging. Therefore, there is need for our intellectual work not to be directed by research agendas set outside the country. We need to reflect on some of the development agencies' popular ideas and question them when necessary.

The "Crisis" of Higher Education and the Prescriptions

Using many examples from throughout the world, the World Bank in the early 1990s analysed problems in the higher education sector. It found that African universities had the most problems but that even universities in the industrial world were not spared. Higher education was found to be heavily dependent on government funding, and unit costs were high relative to other segments of the education system. Since this was an era of widespread fiscal constraints, it followed that education budgets, particularly expenditure per student, became compressed (World Bank 1994: 16). There was a move to-wards greater privatisation of higher education which has transformed uni-versities in many parts of the world. In Britain, for example, the Thatcher "revolution" shook up the British university system, making formerly tenured academics vulnerable and scrapping "unproductive" courses.

In Tanzania, the crisis of higher education was both a crisis of the economy and a crisis of governance. The commendable social services approach could not be sustained by a malfunctioning economy and declining foreign aid, but the crisis was also one of governance. In an economy dominated by parastatals, performance was very poor not only because the parastatals were loss-making, but also because reform was not possible due to entrenched vested interests. The public enterprises which were supposed to be productive were in fact dependent on subsidies from the treasury. The social service sector therefore could not be sustained, and it stated crumbling. It is easy to dismiss the whole system as financially unsustainable without highlighting the issues of governance and management, but these issues do make a difference. The University of Dar es Salaam has had practical experience of this. An institution full of red tape and inefficiency was transformed into an efficient system when Professor Mmari became Vice Chancellor, limited resources notwithstanding.

The 1994 World Bank report identified a number of factors contributing to the crisis of higher education. The first was resource constraints. As the number of students enrolled in higher education institutions rose, adverse macro-economic conditions increased competition for scarce public funds. The result was a sharp decline in real per-student expenditures. The second factor was inadequate staffing. Teachers' salaries had been declining in real terms, and as a result the ability of public higher education institutions to retain qualified staff became a persistent problem. The third factor was deteriorating infrastructure. Higher education managers were concentrating on meeting immediate operating needs, neglecting the maintenance requirements of the physical plant. The fourth factor was the lack of both internal and external efficiency. Internally, there was an inefficient use of existing facilities, while, externally, graduate unemployment increased and there was a decline in research output (World Bank 1994: 16-20).

In Tanzania, the decline in government spending on education coincided with a period of structural adjustment reforms initiated to restore economic growth. Growth was 6 percent in 1979 but fell to just over 4 percent in the early 1980s and to below 4 percent in the 1990s (Johnson 2004). The expansion in student enrolment came only later. In fact the listed 'appallingly' low student enrolment as one of the major problems facing higher education in Tanzania. The other problems which were identified were a gross imbalance in science relative to liberal arts, gender imbalance, poor financing, unregulated and uncontrolled proliferation of tertiary training institutions and a tendency to distort the real worth of academic programs.

There was therefore a difference between the World Bank policy position and the Tanzanian policy position in 1999. Yet, Tanzania has continually been implementing higher education reforms which were already charted out by the World Bank in 1994, based on analysis of the crisis of higher education existing elsewhere. It is clear that the government decision to give education and health a lower priority came with the structural adjustment programmes of the International Monetary Fund (IMF) and the World Bank. One cannot say there was no need for reform in higher education, but the reforms should have arisen from an analysis of the specific Tanzanian situation, not from standardised reform packages which throw away established principles without any remorse. The World Bank's conception of equity, for example, is qualitatively inferior to the principles of equity which had already been achieved in Tanzania. I will return to this issue later, after briefly discussing the World Bank prescriptions which have guided higher education reforms in Tanzania.

The World Bank's reform strategy has four key directions. The first is encouraging greater differentiation of institutions, including the development of private institutions. It is an attack on the traditional model of the European research university, which is seen as too expensive and inappropriate for the developing world. The strategy promotes the establishment of non-university institutions such as polytechnics, short-cycle professional and technical institutes, community colleges and so on, which can be linked with university programmes. It also encourages the growth of private institutions to meet the growing social demand for higher education and to make higher education systems more responsive to changing labour needs.

This strategy is reasonable if indeed the aim is to meet the growing demand for higher education and not to kill the public university. However, the latter seems to be the hidden agenda. In Tanzania, this is reflected in the recent Government Student's Loan Board Act of 2004, passed by parliament despite protests. It is now a complete loan system, and everybody has a right to it, but it is no accident that while student and academic staff at the university protested, the bill won support from the Tanzania Association of Private Universities (TAPU), whose Vice Chancellors and Provosts met in Moshi and urged rapid assent to the bill by the President.

The second key direction of the World Bank reform strategy is to provide incentives for public institutions to diversify sources of funding, including cost sharing with students and linking of government funding to performance. When presented initially, these ideas looked moderate and reasonable. The idea of cost sharing looked like a good idea, especially since "free" services had become completely inefficient and badly distorted by corruption and favouritism. There was also room for more efficient utilisation of resources, given the obvious wastefulness of some services, for example, cafeterias. However, what appeared at first to be a modest cost-sharing initiative soon turned into a full- cost programme. It is evident that in the reforms there is an agenda directed at the eventual privatisation of the public university.

The third pillar of the reforms is the redefinition of the role of government in higher education. It is argued that in most developing countries the extent of government involvement in higher education has far exceeded what is economically efficient. What is recommended is, of course, the expansion of the private sector role in higher education. Indeed, the continued need for support of higher education is justified by the argument that the private sector is unlikely to invest sufficiently in higher education because the returns are mostly long-term. The significance of the role of the university as a source of locally relevant knowledge that can be an alternative to the standardised knowledge imported from outside the country is overlooked from this perspective.

The fourth key direction of the World Bank reforms is to introduce policies explicitly designed to give priority to quality and equity objectives. There are three aspects to this: first, increased quality of teaching and research; second, increased responsiveness of higher education to labour market demands; and third, increased equity. The first two goals are worth pursuing as long as they do not endanger independent thinking and alternative knowledge production. Responsiveness to labour markets is clearly a valid objective, but we need to be clear that university education cannot simply be reduced to job training. The question of equity is more controversial, and here there is hypocrisy on the part of the World Bank. The prescription for greater equity starts with an assertion, which is not well substantiated, that public higher education in the developing world principally benefits the most affluent households who are also the most powerful politically. It is argued that subsidies therefore have to be removed because the children of the well off are the most heavily subsidised by the rest of the society, thus reinforcing their economic and social advantage. What is not clear, however, is how the children of the poor will benefit from the removal of subsidies. If this is to be accomplished through a credit system, the same children from the well off families will continue to dominate. The ongoing controversy over the operations of the government loans board illustrates the issues of contention.

In Tanzania, one important principal of equity over the years has been access to higher education for Tanzanians who have done very well in their secondary studies, regardless of family background or ethnic origin. Many current political leaders and professionals got access to education through this system. Many would not have acquired higher education if the school fees for secondary schools had not been abolished after independence and if university education had not been virtually free. Insofar as it was administered fairly, the Tanzanian system was equalising, in that regardless of their background, children received an education on the basis of good passes. It is simply wrong, at least for the system as it originally operated, to say that higher education was for children of privileged groups. If you came from a privileged background, you obtained a position in higher education because you deserved it by virtue of your grades, not your family's wealth or connections. In the new system, the state will certainly benefit from payments by well-to-do parents, but many children of the poor will miss the opportunity for higher education. It becomes complicated when a poor parent has several talented children capable of pursuing higher studies. The goal of equity might have suffered in recent times due to the serious decline of schools in the rural areas, yet many of the most talented students come from struggling families or are assisted by relatives. Each nation has a practical interest in educating its most talented sons and daughters and a moral responsibility to try to do so. The cutoff point can be debated, but a good percentage at the top need to benefit. Other aspects of equity can be pursued without undermining equity based on merit. Efforts to ensure gender equality in higher education are being taken and are commendable. At present, there is also need to address the declining quality of education in the rural areas, which is marginalising the sons and daughters of peasants.

The Practice and the New Crisis

Since the introduction of structural adjustment programmes and the introduction of cost-sharing in higher education, there has been persistent conflict between the state and university students. If the majority of students come from privileged families, why have they been so vehement against the reforms? Indeed, without their protests, admission to the university would already be based entirely on the ability to fully pay for one's studies. To explain this anomaly, it is important to understand the hidden agenda of the World Bank, which is to promote neo-liberalism. The bank's analytical model underscores the rationale of market-oriented solutions through the use of cost recovery. The market is seen as the most efficient way of allocating resources, whereas alternative analytical models seek to substantiate non-market solutions to the problems of resource allocation in social sectors such as education (Johnson 2004).

The predominant factor in World Bank discourse is economic growth. If you achieve economic growth, then you can invest in education, reduce poverty, promote equity, etc. Indeed, in this model, economic growth is the key to improving social services, but this has to go along with a willingness to invest in those sectors. The World Bank reform strategy has been pursued systematically over the years, but the provision of public higher education has been suffocated. The Government Student Loan Board Act of 2004 is another major step towards that goal. The board will provide loans to cover tuition fees as well as meals and accommodation charges, books, stationery, field practicals and so on, but it will also impose conditions on the loans, demand security and require repayment in installments at the time intervals it deems right. Criminal proceedings will be opened against any beneficiary fails to repay the money. Assurances are given that no capable student will miss out on a loan because of lack of collateral, yet since the first stage of cost sharing, assurances about fairness and equity have been given and have been unscrupulously broken. It is stated that stakeholders have been consulted, but their ideas have not been taken up. The debate by CCM members of parliament was only a smokescreen, as they always vote for government bills unless their personal interests are threatened.

Most tellingly, the implementation of the World Bank reforms has gone together with growing authoritarianism in institutions of higher learning. Students are not heard and their protests are suppressed, while ordinary members of the staff have become spectators when it comes to policy making. They are simply expected to implement what others have decided. We have witnessed the disenfranchisement of members of academic staff. But if the most learned members of society cannot handle democracy, who then can? There are internal measures and pressures which can be used to avoid complacency among staff, but why is it thought that reform can be achieved through the denial of democratic processes?

Generation or Recycling of Knowledge

Many universities now generate income from consultancies and commercial research projects. These activities are beneficial for institutional capacity building as well as for the welfare of participating members and need to be encouraged. At the same time, attracting new paying students is important. When pushed too far, however, these trends have a tendency to undermine the generation of new ideas. Consultancies, for example, can pay well, but in many cases they are limited in generating new knowledge. Clients know what they are looking for, and sometimes they are looking for excuses to justify conclusions which they have already arrived at. Fighting poverty is an example. It has been argued that fighting poverty has become the justification for the prescriptions geared to 'opening up' developing countries to external economic actors and free market rules. It is further argued that World Bank missions come already prepared with their perspectives on the country's poverty situation, their analysis of the country's obstacles to economic growth, their menu of policy options and their views on how to mobilise resources for poverty reduction. Thus there is no "national ownership" of the decision making process; on completion of the "consultation" process, the Poverty Reduction Support Programme (PRSP) has to be jointly assessed by World Bank staff before approval (Jubilee South 2001).

On the question of students, the excessive student numbers are having a disastrous impact on quality and undermining the generation of knowledge by academic staff. To be sure there is an increasing demand for higher education, and the establishment of new private universities needs to be supported. In that case government needs to support private universities. The trend in some neighbouring universities, where heavy teaching is conducted during evening hours, would spell disaster for the generation of new knowledge, as academic staff would be permanently busy teaching and marking scripts. The question which comes up is whether the state is truly interested in facilitating local universities as sources of knowledge which could assist the social transformation of Tanzanian society. When we look at the dominant ideas which influence government decisions and practice, we find that these ideas are not indigenous. We therefore need indigenous knowledge to come from a research agenda which is not dictated from elsewhere.

Conclusion

The days of the traditional university, wholly dependent on government funding, might be over; yet even the most capitalist of countries, the USA, has its list of state universities and offers full scholarships to talented students. In the University of Dar es Salaam and in its public secondary school system, Tanzania had developed an enviable system of selection on the basis of merit. That system produced a public service where recruitment and advancement was largely based on merit and which minimised such ills as ethnicity. The expansion of private universities and privately sponsored students in public universities is commendable in the light of the increasing demand for university education and the needs of development. Attacking the public scholarship system, however, is attacking one of the pillars of the Tanzanian equity system, as talented but economically poor students will miss the chance to pursue higher studies.

References

Johnson, T., 2004, 'The Evaluation of Educational Reforms in Sub-Saharan Africa', *African Symposium*, Vol. 4, No. 1, March.

Jubilee, S., 2001, *The World Bank and the PRSP: Flawed Thinking and Failing Experiences*, (http:// www.focuseb.org/ Ottawa).

World Bank, 1994, *Higher Education: The Lessons of Experience*, Washington DC: World Bank.

5

The University as a Site of Knowledge: The Role of Basic Research

Chachage Seithy L. Chachage

'The scramble to get into college is going to be so terrible in the next few years that students are going to put up with almost anything, even an education.' Barnaby Keeney, President, Brown University (cited in Charlton 1994: 14)

Introduction

On 30 April 2003, the then United States Ambassador to Tanzania, Mr Robert V. Royall, was scheduled to inaugurate a USAID-funded modern transportation engineering laboratory on the University of Dar es Salaam (UDSM) main campus ('The Hill'). This was at a time when the United States and Britain were pouring down thousands of tons of bombs on Iraq. On 29 April 2003, the University of Dar es Salaam Academic Staff Assembly (UDASA) strongly and unreservedly protested against the presence of the Ambassador on the main campus and called upon its members and the university community to boycott the event. UDASA stated that the American and British bombing campaign was

> reducing ... [Iraq] to rubble, and literally disarming children, as the likes of Ali losing their limbs [had] shown'. It also complained that as a result of the bombing 'the great libraries and museums of Iraq went up in flames, destroying the record of over ten centuries of Arab, Islamic and human civilisation.

The UDASA protest did not go down well with the university administration, even though the Tanzanian government was also opposed to the invasion of Iraq, as Parliament had been informed in the same month. The vice-chancellor responded to the UDASA statement through a letter to the chairperson on 9 May 2003. Among other things, the letter questioned whether the statement was not contrary to the right to academic freedom. The vice-chancellor argued:

> A university is a free market of ideas. One would, therefore, have thought that 'un-embedded' intellectuals would have asked, not for a boycott of Ambassador Royall's visit, but for an invitation to him to a discussion/debate/ panel discussion with others holding views different from those of UDASA.

The letter continued: 'Why was this option not exercised? By condemning the US, unheard as is done in the statement, will an invitation to a US government representative to the UDSM for a debate/discussion stand any chance of success?' The letter went on to question even the calibre of the academic members of staff, claiming they were not aware of the implications of their actions. 'Has UDASA reflected', the vice-chancellor asked, 'on what intellectuals elsewhere in the world who read the UDASA statement will conclude about the calibre and quality of intellectuals at UDSM?' Then came the real crunch:

> Would any of the un-embedded intellectuals have their sons, daughters or relatives studying or living in the US or UK? Would one meet any of them standing in queue for a visa to the US or UK? Will any of them neither seek nor accept funding for research, sabbaticals, and other academic pursuits from any of the two countries?

The following year, UDASA and the university administration clashed again, after the administration, on 21 April 2004, suspended all students for 'security' reasons. This followed a two-day boycott of classes in protest against the Student Loans Bill, aimed at introducing the last phase of so-called cost sharing in higher education. On 20 April students had demonstrated against the bill, only to meet the wrath of the state in the form of the police and paramilitary, who broke up the demonstration using excessive force. Many students were wounded or jailed. When UDASA protested against this shabby treatment of the students, the administration questioned its legitimacy as an organisation and the manner in which it conducted itself as far as decision-making was concerned. The administration even challenged UDASA to conduct an opinion poll to ascertain whether its members truly agreed with the positions taken by the organisation, arguing that UDASA lacked even the basic rudiments of strategic planning.

Under such circumstances, can the university still be considered a site of knowledge? Is it possible to undertake basic research in a situation where donors and international financial institutions (IFIs) dominate in every sphere of society and academia? What all the above demonstrates is the fact that there is nothing like academic freedom in the abstract. In the case of our countries, it 'exists fully and concretely for those who control the means of production and circulation of knowledge, whether as a private or state capital; they can decide what to produce and how to produce it' (Ake 1994: 17). The dictum that knowledge is power has been familiar since the times of Francis Bacon, but with rapid advances in information technology in the North, it is said increasingly that knowledge and the capacity to produce it are becoming key economic inputs which at the extreme supersede land, capital and labour.

The 1990 and 1991 Declarations on Academic Freedom

To discuss meaningfully the topic at hand, it is necessary to revisit the context under which two key statements on academic freedom in Africa were produced – the Dar es Salaam Declaration on Academic Freedom and Social Responsibility of Academics (1990) and the Kampala Declaration on Intellectual Freedom and Social Responsibility (1991). The budgetary crises in African states during the late 1970s and 1980s had resulted in governments bowing to the dictates of international financial institutions by liberalising their economies and introducing anti-welfare policies as part of structural adjustment programmes (SAPs). Currency devaluations and sky-rocketing inflation rates had eroded the earnings of the people in general, including academics. Institutions of higher learning had become characterised by the collapse of infrastructure such as libraries, bookstores and research facilities, serious shortages of books, laboratory equipment and research funds, inadequate teaching personnel and poor staff development and motivation.

In this context, working conditions and remuneration in institutions of higher learning verged on the catastrophic. Academic members of staff were migrating to 'greener pastures', including apartheid South Africa, or resorting to outside work such as dubious donor-funded consultancies or even keeping poultry. Classrooms were overcrowded, students were becoming lecturer-dependent (relying on lecture notes and readers' notes) and lecturers were increasingly demoralised. In addition, there was a steady deterioration of social and cultural values on many campuses, with a resurgence of gender-based, racial, nationalist, ethnic, religious and cultural prejudices, amidst an atmosphere of petty antipathies, bad conscience and brutal mediocrity. In the early 1990s, for example, a female student at the University of Dar es Salaam, Revina Mukasa, committed suicide as a result of gender harassment.

There were more and more incidents of violence on campuses, along with a marked tendency for students to regroup themselves in terms of ethnic affiliations. Ethnic affiliations, which were previously unheard of among students in Tanzania, had become necessary; it was claimed, to be a 'survival mechanism'. Students helped each other to cope with the hardships resulting from 'cost-sharing' measures, but only within ethnic groupings.

On the other hand, the deteriorating situation resulted in growing activism on campuses as a result of the growing demands by academics for a living wage and protests by students against the so-called cost-sharing measures. Usually governments in Africa have responded to this activism with the use of force, deploying military and security forces on campuses to 'restore law and order'. In several instances, confrontations between these forces and students or academic staff have led to the closure of campuses. It was in this context that questions about academic freedom and the responsibilities of higher learning institutions and their autonomy were raised. The debates ranged from those focusing mainly on better living and working conditions to those 'concerned more directly with academic freedom and the relationship of the intellectual to society…[and] to those directly and centrally involved in broader democratic struggles' (Diouf and Mamdani 1994: 4).

The Dar es Salaam and Kampala Declarations were not explicit on the role of the universities as sites of knowledge or even on the role of basic research. It seems that these issues were assumed to remain within the context of the traditional objectives of the university – scientific enquiry, pursuit of knowledge and the search for the whole truth in the interest of social transformation and human emancipation. The institutional transformations that were to be introduced in the universities in the 1990s and how these would impinge on knowledge production and research in general were hardly taken aboard, even in subsequent follow-ups on academic freedom (see CODESRIA 1996 and Sall 2000, for example). The issues of vital importance in the discussions in the 1990s remained those of harassment, repression, intimidation, suspensions, remuneration and freedom of expression, association, demonstration and assembly.

Postmodernism, Knowledge, Research and Neoliberalism

The French postmodernist Jean-François Lyotard published a book in 1979 which was translated into English in 1984 as *The Postmodern Condition: A Report on Knowledge*. In this work, Lyotard accounted for the changing nature of knowledge in the advanced capitalist societies and reassessed the role of the universities, given the computerisation process in those societies. His working hypothesis was that 'the status of knowledge is altered as societies enter what is known as the post-industrial age and cultures enter what is known as the postmodern age' (Lyotard 1984: 3). The term 'postmodern condition' was used to describe the state of knowledge and the problem of its legitimation, following what Lyotard considered to be the transformations that had been taking place in those countries since the 1950s.

According to Lyotard, the Enlightenment project and its metanarratives concerning meaning, truth and emancipation, which had been used to legitimate both the rules of knowledge and the foundations of modern institutions, besides laying down the game rules for science, literature and the arts, had reached a crisis in the most highly developed societies. The 'postmodern condition' was defined by 'incredulity toward metanarratives' (Lyotard 1984: xxiv). By this phrase Lyotard meant to point to 'the obsolescence of the metanarrative apparatus of legitimation' to which corresponds 'the crisis of metaphysical philosophy and of the university institution' (Lyotard 1984: xxiii).

Lyotard further claimed that knowledge was increasingly becoming the major force of production and was increasingly becoming translated into quantities of information, with a corresponding reorientation in the process of research. He claimed that 'the miniaturization and commercialization of machines is already changing the way in which learning is acquired, classified, made available, and exploited' (Lyotard 1984: 4). Knowledge in computerised societies was becoming 'exteriorised' from knowers, and the age-old notion of knowledge and pedagogy being inextricably linked was being replaced by a new view of knowledge as a commodity: 'Knowledge is and will be produced in order to be sold, it is and will be consumed in order to be valorized in a new production: in both cases, the goal is exchange. Knowledge ceases to be an end in itself, it loses its "use-value" ...' (Lyotard 1984: 4-5).

According to Lyotard, knowledge in the form of informational commodity had become indispensable to productive power: 'It is conceivable that the nation-states will one day fight for control of information, just as they battled in the past for control over territory, and afterwards for control and access to and exploitation of raw materials and cheap labour' (Lyotard: 5). In this context, the idea that 'learning falls within the purview of the State, as the mind or brain of society' was giving way to the idea that 'society exists and progresses only if messages circulating within it are rich in information and easy to decode' (Lyotard 1984: 5). In sum:

> We may thus expect a thorough exteriorization of knowledge with respect to the 'knower', at whatever point he or she may occupy in the knowledge process. The old principle that the acquisition of knowledge is indissociable from the training *(Bildung)* of minds, or even of individuals, is becoming obsolete and will become ever more so. The relationships of the suppliers and users of knowledge to the knowledge they supply and use is now tending, and will increasingly tend, to assume the form already taken by the relationship of

commodity producers and consumers to the commodities they produce and consume – that is, the form of value (Lyotard 1984: 4-5).

In the computer age, with the state playing more of a regulatory role, the power to make decisions will be determined by the question of access to information. Eventually academics will not be needed, since much of the work they undertake will be taken over by computerised data network systems.

Lyotard was essentially acknowledging the omnipotence of the free-market economy.

The university, with all its faculties and intellectual specialisations, becomes untenable because of the new nature of knowledge – cyberspace information processing which quantifies knowledge according to computer logic. For postmodernists, the knower has been transformed into a consumer of knowledge. Perhaps these claims by Lyotard, which were celebrated in Europe and exerted profound influence among other postmodernists, could have remained a European academic fad, except for the fact they reinforced the ideas developed by the theorists of 'post-industrial society', such as Touraine (1971) and Bell (1974) on information/knowledge workers. These theorists argued that industrial society was moving from a goods-producing to a service economy and was characterised by the pre-eminence of the professional and technical class and the widespread diffusion of 'intellectual technology'. After the 1968 student revolts in Europe Touraine predicted the possibility of deepening conflicts between students and teachers upholding the humanistic values of liberal education on the one hand and, on the other hand, those who control the technocratic apparatuses and are dedicated to economic growth.

Above all, Lyotard's claims were being given credence and substance by developments in science – the new information technology (global cyberspace), the new cosmologies developed by conventionalists (the theory of everything) and the developments in genetic science (the human genome project). They also coincided with the rise of neo-liberal politics with the ascendancy of Pope John Paul II (Karol Wojtyla in 1978), President Ronald Reagan (1980) and Prime Minister Margaret Thatcher (1981) and the collapse of the Berlin Wall in 1989, which signaled the complete triumph of the market economy. African and other developing countries were forced to structurally adjust their economies, adopt market-oriented policies and privatise public enterprises. With the rise of computer technology, cellular phones, modems and faxes, the world's financial markets became hooked up into a system of 24-hour non-stop trading. Take-over specialists bought and sold enterprises all over the world, making tens of thousands of workers redundant and countless stockholders rich, regardless of the long-term economic goals of a country.

The determinists in genetic science, sponsored by the multibillion-dollar Human Genome Project, which aimed to map and analyse the complete genetic blueprint of human beings, lent weight to the idea that human beings are pre-determined, whether in terms of intelligence, free market entrepreneurship, sexuality, male dominance, etc. Thus the project worked to legitimise the status quo of existing inequalities and forms of domination. Meanwhile, as far as physics was concerned, theories of chaos and complexity demolished the notion of control and certainty in science. Conventionalists claimed that scientific methods are just myths and that scientific knowledge is manufactured. Paul Feyeraband (1971: 5) had earlier explicitly argued that the 'only principle that does not exhibit progress is: anything goes .... Without chaos, no knowledge. Without a frequent dismissal of reason, no progress'.

As a 1994 European Union White Paper pointed out, there has been an increasing shift from the kind of society where formal learning occurs once-off towards one in which education does not stop after one has obtained a qualification. Thus, both public and private organisations are increasingly taking on the continuing education of their members as a major responsibility. The South African National Commission for Higher Education therefore concludes:

> This means that higher education institutions will no longer have a monopoly on the transmission of knowledge, which will become increasingly diversified, with the higher education institution being only one of many organisations competing for the education/training market (NCHE 1996: 39).

In such an environment, if higher education institutions are not to be marginalised, they are going to have to develop partnerships with both private and public-sector organisations .

Neo-liberalism and Institutional Transformation in Tanzania

Broadly, whatever the misgivings some may have, post-independence Tanzanian nation-building was based on welfare policies that assumed the public provision of health, education, water, etc. This was reflected even in the conception of what the university and other institutions of higher learning were all about. According to Nyerere (1973: 192-3), the university was an institution where people's minds should be 'trained for clear thinking, for independent thinking, for analysis and for problem solving at the highest level. This is the meaning of 'a university' anywhere in the world.' Thus, the university's role was threefold: to transmit advanced knowledge from one generation to another 'so that this can serve either as a basis of action, or as a springboard for further research', to advance the frontiers of knowledge 'through its possession of good library and laboratory facilities', and finally to provide high-level manpower to society. All three are necessary: 'a university which attempts to prohibit any one of [these functions] would die – it would cease to be a university' (Nyerere 1973: 193). For Nyerere, universities in developing countries have exactly the same high responsibility towards themselves and their societies:

> Thus our university, like all others worthy of the name, must provide the facilities and the opportunities for the highest intellectually enquiry. It must encourage and challenge its students to develop their powers of constructive thinking. It must encourage its academic staff to do original research and to play a full part in promoting intelligent discussion of issues of human concern. It must do all these things because they are part of being a university; they are part of its reason for existence (Nyerere 1973: 197).

In keeping with this vision, post-independence education policies in Tanzania were premised on the provision of education, especially higher education, as the basis for social and economic development, with the state playing the central role.

However, the neo-liberal policies which were developed in the 1980s to cope with the crisis that had begun to face African economies since the 1970s argued that developing countries, with their abundant supply of unskilled labour, had a comparative advantage in the production of labour-intensive goods and services.[1] With increased free trade, this argument held, the wages of unskilled labour would increase in these countries, since goods produced by unskilled labour in the developed countries would face competition from those from developing countries, given the scarcity of unskilled labour in the former. Therefore free markets and competition would enhance technological progress and lead to high-quality, sustained growth in the developing countries (Michalopoulos 1987: 24). Within this context the World Bank produced a number of studies on education in Africa from the mid-1980s on (World Bank 1985, 1986, 1988, 1989, 1990a, 1991; Kelly 1991) calling for drastic reductions in state funding of higher education in Africa on the pretext of promoting higher efficiency and more egalitarian distribution of resources.

These studies claimed that the social return on public investment in primary education was 28 per cent, while that on tertiary education was only 13 per cent. They also argued that the return on *private* investment in higher education was as high as 32 per cent. The studies concluded that individual university graduates received about 2.5 times more income over outlay than the government but received 34 times more from the government than what primary students received. Accordingly, they concluded, education financing was unbalanced, and investment in higher education was inefficient. In the words of Michael Kelly (1991: 7), 'wastage, proliferation of small institutions, excessively large (especially non-teaching) staff and the nearly universal policy of charging no fees all contribute to high costs'.

The studies also argued that the distribution of education expenditure was very inegalitarian. For example, they claimed that 40 per cent of university students came from white-collar families (professionals, government employees and corporate employees). White-collar families represented only 6 percent of the population but appropriated about 27 per cent of public education expenditure. Thus, rather than alleviating poverty, public expenditure in higher education, it was claimed, was increasing it. The World Development Report of 1990 identified the most critical elements of poverty reduction as labour-intensive growth, investment in human capital and safety nets for the poor. It emphasised the need for growth that is labour-intensive and removes distortions in labour markets. This was a time when many donor agencies had shifted their support to projects promising short-term payoffs, which were mostly administered by NGOs whose success did not depend on high-level skills, such as technical skills or PhDs. This approach reinforced the shift away from higher education as a development priority (Doss et al. 2004: 2).

At a World Bank meeting of African vice-chancellors in Harare in 1988, it was even claimed that Africa's need for university education to fill white-collar jobs could be met by overseas education institutions, so that resources could be channelled to primary, secondary and vocational education. The assumption was that African workers were destined for a long time to remain unskilled workers. This was the position of the World Bank's first Africa-specific education policy paper, *Education in Sub-Saharan Africa: Policies for Adjustment, Revitalisation and Expansion* (1988). The paper was produced at a time when the bank's lending for the social sector was constrained to make room for SAPs lending in what the bank considered to be productive sectors. The main thrust of this policy was that higher education was too expensive and mainly favoured better-off population groups at the expense of primary and secondary education for the majority.

Since there was resistance from the institutions of higher learning, the World Bank called for a restructuring of education, so that there could be public cost-recovery and reallocation of government spending towards levels with the highest social returns. This, according to the World Bank, would promote higher efficiency and more egalitarian distribution of education resources. The bank was of the view that the higher education system should be made to operate at the lowest possible public cost and that higher-education institutions should exist by virtue of being 'viable' and 'efficient'. By viability was meant the institutions 'producing' for the 'market' and paying for themselves. The introduction of cost-sharing was part of this package. By efficiency was meant revising syllabi to ensure 'products' better suited for the market. The World Bank envisioned a network of market-oriented 'centres of excellence' replacing the present university systems. In the view of the World Bank education was bound up with the development of the overall economy. The crucial and determining factor was the question of employment (and unemployment), since educational levels have an effect on employability. Rhetoric aside, this was an expression in a subtle way of the view that universities should be turned into vocational schools in all but name!

According to the World Bank, the multiple changes in economies, cultures and communication systems under globalisation call for greater flexibility in production to meet increasingly diverse global consumer needs. This flexibility can be attained by using new computer-led technologies and employing a more educated labour force in more participatory forms of work organisation. This has led to an increased need for a multi-skilled labour force that can adapt to new technologies and the continuous deployment of new knowledge. The world is entering a new stage – that of the 'knowledge society' – in which productivity is increasingly becoming dependent on knowledge as a form of symbolic capital. Since higher-learning institutions are the natural habitat of specialised knowledge, they should therefore play a central role. The role of higher-learning institutions in Africa becomes one of producing skilled professionals and knowledge workers who can compete internationally.

Within this context, higher education, like other public services, was increasingly being drawn into the world market. For example, it was claimed that students were becoming consumers free to choose the best courses and that there was big money to be made by private firms. Higher education had therefore become a commodity. The income from foreign students in Organisation for Economic Cooperation and Development (OECD) member countries topped USD 30 billion in 1999. Even the World Trade Organisation (WTO) has turned its attention to this sector; the General Agreement on Trade in Services (GATS) has included higher education on the list of services to be privatised since 1994. The negotiations on facilitating the flow of students and educational resources and on establishing colleges and campuses in foreign countries were planned to be completed by 2005.

In terms of financial resources, public universities now had to compete with many other institutions. The changing forms of knowledge dissemination, and the entry of a plethora of private and public institutions performing the same work, ended universities' knowledge 'monopoly'. As far as research was concerned, it was claimed that, given the globalising trends, universities could no longer claim to be the leading sites of knowledge production. Their pre-eminent role had been eroded by multinational and private sector research laboratories, scientific and cultural councils, research councils and agencies and a host of individual and commercial organisations. Within this context, the separation between theoretical (basic) and applied knowledge, it was claimed, was being contested both by the new forms of knowledge production and by new management models of research.

In the light of these developments internationally, and the changing conception of the role of the university that they have given rise to, one can begin to make sense of the transformations that began to take place in the University of Dar es Salaam in the 1990s. The University of Dar es Salaam started reviewing its mission, objectives and activities in 1991, given that donors had shown a willingness to fund those transformations. The *raison d'être* for the review, it was claimed, was the fact that since 1985 Tanzanian society had undergone major changes politically and economically. The economy had changed from centralised to market-oriented, and the political system had changed from a one-party to multi-party. As the university administration concluded, 'the existing capacities of the university were seen to be inadequate in meeting the increasing demand, thus calling for new and more efficient modes of delivery and strategic thinking' (UDSM 2004: 2).

Basically, the thinking behind the review was in line with the policies that were being pushed by the World Bank and that had already been accepted by the government of Tanzania. UDASA's critical appraisal of these ideas in 1993, and of the issue of cost-sharing proposed by the university administration, fell on deaf ears. The administration went ahead with launching the Institutional Transformation Programme (ITP) 1993–2008, which aimed to analyse institutional strengths and weaknesses, find ways to reduce the costs of training students, agitate for a 'flexible' University Act to improve the 'autonomy' of the institution and, finally, improve the working conditions and environment for staff and students.

With the implementation of the ITP over the years, student enrolment increased from 2,898 in 1995 to 8,411 in 2002 and to almost 14,000 by 2004. The proportion of female students increased from 15.9 per cent in 1995 to 31 per cent in 2004. The increase in enrolment resulted from an increased number of private students rather than from more government sponsorship. At another level, the university privatised and outsourced several functions and had reduced the number of support staff by 1,013 by June 2002. It increased to some extent the space for teaching and student accommodation and introduced new training programmes and new management units. ICT infrastructure and capacity were enhanced, as were awareness and utilisation of ICT resources. The university also hived off units involved in the provision of services such as catering, accommodation, cleaning, transportation, etc., created a 'conducive environment for outsiders to invest on university lands' and adopted contract employment as the norm instead of employment on permanent and pensionable terms (UDSM 2004: 4-5). Over the past few years the university has also embarked on the introduction of 'programmes of excellence' that aim for multi-disciplinarity and that respond to job markets. A more corporate institutional culture has also been promoted.

All these transformations are aimed at responding both to global trends and the national goals advocated in the Tanzania Vision 2025, the Poverty Reduction Strategy Paper, the Higher Education Sub-Master Plan, the Science and Technology Sub-Master Plan, the Civil Service Reform Programme, the National ICT Policy, etc. The stakeholders in the implementation of the transformations are the government, the university management, the university council, the Programme Steering Committee, the major university offices, the boards of colleges, faculties, institutes and major departments, the private sector and the 'development partners' (donors). Staff and students are the 'beneficiaries'.

As a result of this process, the University of Dar es Salaam has reached a point where the production of 'marketable goods' – works, courses and graduates – is given priority over academic excellence, and where academic excellence is defined, in the narrow terms of policy makers, as marketability of courses and 'outputs'. With these corporate strategic goals in place until at least 2013, it would seem that the University of Dar es Salaam is behaving like Rip Van Winkle. For example, the University of Cape Town, which introduced similar institutional transformations in the mid-1990s, abandoned them in 2001 after recognising the dangers they posed as far as knowledge production and dissemination are concerned. More recently, the World Bank itself has made an about-turn regarding its policies on higher education. Since 2000 the bank has produced reports which have suddenly rediscovered the centrality of education and, in particular tertiary education, for 'the creation of intellectual capacity on which knowledge production utilisation depend and to the promotion of lifelong-learning practices necessary for updating people's knowledge and skills' (cited in Sall 2004: 179). Moving away from the higher-education model of the 1980s and 1990s, the bank has begun talking about alternative models with a re-emphasis on the traditional forms of public higher education and knowledge production (Sall 2004: 180). It is recognising that the public university as conceptualised in the 1960s provided the services it was expected of it, and that the social value of its degrees was quite high, even in times of crisis. It is recognising that, with the policies of the 1980s and 1990s, there was hardly any basic research being undertaken and universities had ceased being sites of knowledge production in anything but name.

Conclusion

Under the present conditions, academic freedom belongs to those who control and own the means of production of knowledge and its dissemination, not those who actually generate and disseminate the knowledge. With international financial institutions and donors playing a central role, the trend has been towards privatisation of educational processes, programmes and responsibilities while at the same time strengthening state control. The language has changed: students have been redefined as 'consumers' or 'customers', and universities have become 'providers'. The officials and administrators use the language of 'inputs', 'outputs' and 'throughputs', and any notion that education serves some form of collective public good has been removed.

Basic research, as traditionally defined, is a focused, systematic study undertaken to discover new knowledge or interpretations and establish facts or principles in a particular field. This has always been differentiated from applied research, which though also a focused, systematic study, is done in order to discover the problem-solving applications of the knowledge established by basic research. However, since the current transformations in higher education began, university staff members have either been engaged as 'counterparts' (spare parts) by researchers from Europe and the US, basically as enumerators, or at best they have survived on consultancies guided by external terms of reference. Even where it has been possible to undertake research independently, this has been possible mainly through new research centres or programmes such as the Research in Poverty Alleviation (REPOA) and the Economic and Social Research Foundation (ESRF) which have been established through donor funding to cater for the interests of the current economic dispensation.

At the University of Dar es Salaam, no distinction is now made between consultancies and independent research; they are both 'research'. Moreover, as far as most are concerned, a research is only genuine when it involves field work and questionnaires. It is not surprising, therefore, that some lecturers teach focus group discussions (FGD) and rapid rural appraisals as research methods. These are eclectic methods that have been developed by donor agencies for purposes of collecting data in a short period in order to make quick decisions on a project. There are local academics who have learnt the same tricks of academic entrepreneurship as their colleagues of the Atlantic world and who have found a fertile ground for prospering in these circumstances of anti-foundationalism and sophistry expressed in the form of relativism. Some of them have been enjoying affluent styles of living using grants from so-called applied branches of science and research, which are claimed to be applications and developments of the 'pure' knowledge of the academy. There are those who have even been employed by branches of the state and industry, thus making 'research' a big business. This tendency for academic entrepreneurs to emerge has over the years been accompanied by the prominence of centres, bureaus, institutes, programme-based teaching, etc.

Under such circumstances, a successful academic is not one whose research is acceptable to his or her discipline or relevant to human needs, but one whose research is capable of attracting the greatest funds or who controls a research institution capable of distancing itself from the purely teaching structure of the faculties and departments. The most successful have been those employed to advise the government, the international financial institutions and other donors. Financial sponsors are the ones who determine the forms of knowledge, and accepted knowledge has over the years come to be defined as knowledge produced by 'research technicians' or 'professional researchers' rather than genuine scientists. The academic entrepreneurs have reduced knowledge to 'pragmatic' teaching programmes and research on practical concerns.

In this way, the 'stakeholders' have been able to proclaim that 'in such a worldwide informational economy, investment in what is called "human capital" becomes strategic [and] universities become fundamental tools for development' (Castells 1993: 66). They have further proclaimed that knowledge is increasingly no longer a cognitive appropriation of socially determined material transformations for life processes, but instead has become simply a post-industrial force of production, since the real substance of knowledge is informed by developments in science (global cyberspace, theories of everything and progress in genetics and its aims) and the triumph of liberal democracy and a free-market economy. The world has therefore entered an era in which cosmologies of the human subject are not the real thing, since technology and economics have fused under labels such as 'computer economy', 'electronic services' and so on. In sum it is an era of the celebration of the 'end of history' (as Fukuyama famously put it), even while all *other* histories are excluded.

Popular academic and political thinking in Tanzania, and Africa generally, has increasingly ceased to debate emancipationist politics, politics which would lead to the transformation of societies and help people to reach a stage where others' humanity is not contested. Any critique of social realities from the point of view of liberation has become less fashionable. The most fashionable debates are around issues of how African countries can best be 'globalised' as an answer to welfarism, nationalism, socialism and so on. This celebration of the dehumanisation and desocialisation of relationships has been internalised by some academics, so that the concept of the university as an institution in which the faculties are central and the administration plays a supportive role has been reversed. The administration is now the university and the faculties are mere subsidiaries, as in business organisations!

In such an environment, education becomes only a matter of the pursuit and provision of degrees and certificates. Career advancement, not the production of knowledge, becomes the key academic goal, to the extent that it is even possible to marginalise good scholarship and research. This situation becomes an excuse for some academics to pursue private interests to the neglect of public and social responsibilities and, increasingly, there arises a category of academics that live *off* the academy rather than *for* it. The university becomes just another way of getting ahead in the world, economically or otherwise, since there is a market of donors, NGOs, international donor organisations and consulting firms to which one can vend his or her 're-search' skills. In the name of responding to international imperatives, these academics accept the transformation of education from outside the academy based on the findings of consultants who may have little understanding of the difference between universities and corporations.

It is only with the recognition that universities can neither function like government departments nor like businesses that the central issues of knowledge production and basic research can be brought to the fore again. Mahmood Mamdani has pointed out that the reason universities cannot function like governments or businesses is because they are not limited by the short-term considerations of winning votes or making profits. Universities therefore have a unique freedom which gives them the capacity for longer-term research. The value of such research is not measurable in monetary terms, but by its significance to society, if it expands options for a secure and independent future. It is for this reason that higher education has never been profitable anywhere in the world and has always depended on heavy social subsidy (Sall 2004: 203-4).

If the value of higher education is indeed tied to the job market, then it would be logical to simply close universities in developing countries, as there is already too much unemployment! Why train more and more people who will only end up becoming unemployed? Moreover, to tie the whole question of education to the market is to go against the whole essence of human dignity, since what is disregarded here is the fact that education is a fundamental human right. Once upon a time slaves were denied the right to learn how to read and write on the pretext that plantation work did not require them to have such skills. When they were turned into workers, they were told that all they required was simply vocational or technical skills for particular utilitarian ends. They were not supposed to be trained so as to be able to think! That is how colonial education was modelled, and it is this type of education which is being encouraged again today, training in skills but not in thinking. We have become colonial subjects again.

Because education is geared towards the market, students – and even lecturers, I would argue – do not have reading and writing habits, except for utilitarian or bread-and-butter questions, that is, to pass examinations, get a job or a promotion, etc. Nobody wants to go beyond the classroom materials. When it is then claimed that education standards are falling because people are not able to speak or write properly in English, knowledge is being reduced to the question of language. But how does one master any language in this world without using it constantly in reading and writing? The question is pertinent for those of us who would like to consider ourselves 'knowledge-able' without ever visiting libraries or having a single book in our homes (although, of course, the TV or copies of tabloids will definitely be there).

The issue is that conceptualisations of change in the education sector today do not start from the point of view of the problems facing people and their history, or how to make education effective in improving the human condition, but how to create slaves for Mr Money Bags. The debate is no longer about how to bring about forms of knowledge that enhance the chances of mutual survival by dealing with the problems facing humanity, but how our economies and societies can effectively compete and be integrated further into the global economy. It is hardly recognised that even the so-called revolution in communication so beloved by market fundamentalists has itself ignited an awareness of the problems facing humanity locally, regionally and internationally. The fundamental issues of transformation in education, therefore, need to deal with the extent to which the education system is playing its role in dealing with societal problems. This is the social responsibility of any education system worth the name, and it is only from this position that we can justify demands for academic freedom among students and lecturers.

From this point of view, the search should be for an education system that equips people with the necessary tools to create or acquire knowledge and concepts necessary for the survival of the human race in this rapidly changing world. In other words, it is the search for those concepts that enhance emancipationist and transformational modes of social activity. Such forms of knowledge and concepts definitely go beyond the job market's 'person power requirements'. Job markets and markets in general are a constraint on creativity, scientific inquiry, fidelity to the pursuit of truth and intellectual freedom in general. The academy's accommodation to market forces and global forces is nothing more than an ideologically determined position which would like to turn the university into a supermarket without any long-term consideration of national and societal needs. The historical experience in Africa requires a greater ferment of ideas and a more intense sense of commitment to social transformation and human emancipation than ever before. Taking such a position means viewing education from the point of view of fundamental human and peoples' rights. An equitable provision of education cannot be guaranteed if the link between the education institutions and the society is simply a matter of finance. There is nothing like 'free' education or social services in the world, as those who advocate the commercialisation or privatisation of social services want the world to believe. All governments in the world derive their revenue from taxation. It is for this reason that they are supposed to be responsible for the provision of social services and infrastructure. In other words it is society, not governments, that finance social services. Therefore to talk of free services is to mask the truth. To talk about government assistance (or so-called cost-sharing) to those who cannot afford it is a mystification, since those who cannot pay are the majority. Simply put, an education system that treats knowledge production as an industry tends to reinforce inequalities and hierarchisation.

What is important is to search for those responses that would define us in this world, where even our very humanity is questioned. In our situation (given the nature of the problems facing the mass of the people) an intellectual must have a social and historical context. He or she cannot be just a free-floating agent but must be capable of reflecting upon and crystallising the woes and concerns of the masses of Africa – those who are marginalised, exploited and oppressed. The social responsibility of intellectuals lies in the rehabilitation of those academic practices which are sensitive to human predicaments, committed to responding to societal needs by engaging in critical inquiry and analysis and dedicated to championing social forms and organisations capable of fulfilling the needs of the human community as a whole.

Any so-called intellectual who takes it for granted that there is no alternative to the dominant forms of thinking about how the world is, anyone who takes 'for granted that maximum growth, and therefore productivity and competitiveness, are the ultimate and sole goals of human action; or that economic forces cannot be resisted' (Bourdieu 1998: 30), should be called to account. We cannot accept as inevitable the reduction of the state, the removal of the notion of public interests and the destruction of all philosophical foundations of welfarism and collective responsibility towards poverty, misery, sickness, misfortune, etc. on the pretext of reducing the costs of investors and creating an 'enabling environment' for the market.

If universities and their intellectual communities are to remain relevant and socially responsible, they must take the lead in revolting against those notions that treat knowledge and education as private goods and that result in the perpetuation of abuse, prejudices, mediocrity and regressive and repressive interests wrapped in forms of 'universalism of the West'. The precondition for any meaningful renewal of a genuine search for authentic forms of knowledge is the existence of a body of critical intellectuals committed to being radical witnesses on behalf of those who sleep with empty bellies and children who have never experienced childhood because they have to wield guns at tender age. Such an intellectual body must avoid the unwitting pitfall of the demolition of metanarratives, as is the fashion now, or the simple application and use of models. It must win the intellectual high ground for theoretical independence. It is therefore necessary to take philosophy seriously, as the discipline that has traditionally underwritten what constitutes science (or knowledge in general) and determined which political practices are legitimate (Bhaskar 1989: 1). Such a community must be in a position to interrogate the various ontologies in the world, the kind of accounts of the world they give and their status in Africa. For us it is those emancipatory forms of knowledge which should inform our practices, those forms of knowledge which are oriented to human well-being and environmentally sustainable ways of life. Against all the cynicism established by social Darwinism (the cult of the of winner), we must stand against the destruction of those ideals associated with public service, equality of rights and equal access to education, health, culture, research, art, etc. This is the basis of any meaningful renewal of our universities as sites of knowledge and research.

In sum, under the present circumstances, the quest for academic freedom as a right for the producers of knowledge is only meaningful if the universities and their academic members renew their commitment to the public good, which has always been the bedrock of any university worth the name. It is also in this way that public investments in higher education can be justified. It is by offering the best education, knowledge and research which address issues of public interest and the problems facing the people. Only by fulfilling the public trust as weavers of the social fabric and upholders of the highest ethical dimensions of human life can institutions of higher learning reclaim their position in society and the world at large. Rather than supplant the traditional role of training minds and producing thinkers, the new technological revolutions should be made to enhance this role. If there are no thinkers and people who are innovative, creative and original, who is going to advance these technologies further and use them for human good?

Note

1. Most of the following argument is based on my article, 'Social Policy and Development in East Africa: The Case of Education and Labour Markets' in *Social Policy in the Development Context: Africa and the Challenge of Social Policy*, UNRISD, 2003.

References

Ake, C., 1994, 'Academic Freedom and Material Base' in M. Diouf and M. Mamdani, eds., *Academic Freedom in Africa*, Dakar: CODESRIA.

Bell, D., 1974, *The Coming of the Post-Industrial Society: A Venture in Social Forecasting*, London: Heinemann.

Bhaskar, R., 1989, *Reclaiming Reality: A Critical Introduction to Contemporary Philosophy*, London: Verso.

Bourdieu, P., 1998, *Acts of Resistance: Against the New Myths of Our Time,* Cambridge: Polity Press.

Castells, M., 1993, 'The Informational Economy and the New Division of Labour', in M. Carnoy, et al., eds., *The New Global Economy in the Information Age: Reflections on our Changing World,* University Park, PA: Pennsylvania State University Press.

Charlton, J., ed., 1994, *A Little Learning is a Dangerous Thing: 600 Wise and Witty Observations for Students, Teachers and Other Survivors of Higher Education,* London: Robert Hale.

CODESRIA, 2000, *The State of Academic Freedom in Africa*, Dakar: CODESRIA.

Diouf, M. and Mamdani, M., eds., 1994, *Academic Freedom in Africa*, Dakar: CODESRIA.

Doss, S. E., Robert, E. and Ruther, N. L., 2004, 'Introduction and Overview', *Journal of Higher Education in Africa*, 2 (No. 1).

Feyeraband, P. K., 1971, *Against Method*, London: New Left Books.

Kelly, M., 1991, *Education in a Declining Economy: The Case of Zambia, 1975-1985,* Washington DC: World Bank.

Lyotard, J., 1984, *The Postmodern Condition: A Report on Knowledge*, Manchester: Manchester University Press.

Michalopoulos, C., 1987, 'World Bank Programmes for Adjustment and Growth', in V. Gorbo, et al, eds., *Growth-Oriented Adjustment Programmes*, Washington DC: World Bank.

NCHE, 1996, *A Framework for Transformation of Higher Education System, Governance and Funding,* Pretoria: National Commission for Higher Education.

Nyerere, J. K., 1973, *Freedom and Development,* Nairobi: Oxford University Press.

Sall, E., 1996, *Women in Academia: Gender and Academic Freedom in Africa*, Dakar: CODESRIA.

Sall, E., 2004, 'Alternative Models to Traditional Higher Education: Market Demand, Networks, and Private Sector Challenges', in *Journal of Higher Education in Africa* 2, No 1.

Touraine, A., 1971, *The Post-Industrial Society*, New York: Random House.

UDSM, 2004, *Corporate Strategic Planning, 2004-2013,* Dar es Salaam: University of Dar es Salaam, July.

World Bank, 1985, *Issues Related to Higher Education in Su-Saharan Africa,* Washington DC: World Bank.

World Bank, 1986, *Financing Education in Developing Countries,* Washington DC: World Bank.

World Bank, 1988, *Education in Sub-Saharan Africa: Policies for Adjustment, Revitalization, and Expansion,* Washington DC: World Bank.

World Bank, 1989, *Sub-Saharan Africa: From Crisis to Sustainable Growth,* Washington DC: World Bank.

World Bank, 1990a, *World Development Report 1999: Poverty,* Washington DC: World Bank.

World Bank, 1990b, *Why Educational Policies Can Fail: An Overview of Selected African Experiences,* Washington DC: World Bank.

World Bank, 1990c, *Primary Education,* Policy Paper, Washington DC: World Bank.

World Bank, 1991a, *Education and Adjustment: A Review of the Literature,* Washington DC: World Bank.

World Bank, 1991b, *The African Capacity Building Initiative: Towards Improved Policy Analysis and Development Management in Sub-Saharan Africa,* Washington DC: World Bank.

6

The Obligation of the State and Communities in the Provision of Higher Education

Mwajabu K. Possi

Introduction

Higher education in Tanzania is said to be in crisis by many members of society. There have been demands for reforms by people from all walks of life, including many public figures. Recently, comments published in one of the newspapers by a very highly positioned citizen alleged that graduates from the University of Dar es Salaam are unable to compete in the world of work. Among the reasons cited for the alleged deterioration in the quality of higher education are the shortage (or unavailability) of teaching materials and facilities. Other reasons include the increasing numbers of students (admitted without taking into consideration the availability of space and of material and human resources) and the use of inappropriate teaching methodologies due to large class sizes. At the same time, minority groups such as women, people with disabilities and those from what I would call "unreached" communities have been left even further behind in higher education. According to the Minister of Community, Gender and Children, females constituted only 21 percent of students in science and 5.3 percent in architecture in 2004/05. Such figures show that there is still a huge task ahead as far as enrolment of women in higher education is concerned.

The following questions are commonly raised by "consumers" of our products. Is there something wrong with the inputs in terms of the type of students enrolled, the curricula used, the teaching and learning materials, the qualifications of teaching staff, the learning environments etc? Do we blame the problems on the teaching and learning processes, the teaching techniques used in our lecture theatres, seminar rooms, practicals and so on? Can it be that the "outputs", our graduates, are not "selling" out there in terms of their knowledge and social validity? Obviously, if the education being provided is not socially valid and lacks content validity from the point of view of society, it may as well be considered obsolete and meaningless. A critical eye and brain have to be used here. More needs to be done as far as the obligations of the state, the universities and members of the community are concerned. Without the involvement of the state and members of the community, not much is going to be realised. They both have to own the process of higher education.

The Role of Higher Education

Education is concerned with the transfer of knowledge from one individual or environment to the other, leading to a relatively permanent change in cognitive, psychomotor and affective behaviour. It is through education that the individual or environment changes for the better, leading to improvements in both thinking and acting. It is believed that if a person's behaviour does not change after training, no learning can have taken place. The process of education results in individuals possessing knowledge and skills that assist them in their lives. Education therefore prepares individuals for competition in the world of work. It enables them have career options, to be independent and to respond to various challenges. Thus education emancipates individuals and instills freedom in thinking. It also enables them to become socially responsible to the community they live in. This is why countries that do not invest sufficiently in education, such as Tanzania, lack development and become stagnant. Higher education is particularly important because it is meant to produce the "cream" of thinkers – the vanguard of development.

Clearly, it is an obligation of the state and community to provide its citizens with education that instills in them the knowledge and skills that will assist them to thrive and participate in national development. The roles played by the state and various communities are therefore crucial for the provision of higher education. However, in practice the provision of higher education in any country is influenced by a host of factors. Ishumi (2000) asserts that access to education is governed by several parameters including physical barriers, financial barriers, legal and regulatory provisions, availability of supply and the packaging of curricula. These factors influence both the quality and quantity of education provided to learners.

Any caring society must ensure that its members get the best possible education both qualitatively and quantitative. This is to say that all citizens must have fair access to education according to their needs and abilities and that the education services should be equally distributed. At a qualitative level the state and members of the community must be responsible and ensure that there are skilled graduates who are socially responsible members of society for the required social, moral, cognitive and economic development (Possi 2003). The members of society should access education without barriers, and therefore there have to be laws and regulations governing and guiding the provision of education. In addition the teaching and learning materials and techniques must be relevant to the members of the community.

Higher Education Policy in Tanzania

Tanzania has two clearly distinct levels of training institutions in higher education provision – normal academic full-professional training and intermediate professional education and training institutions – which include both university and non-university training institutions with different missions, objectives and curricular orientations. There are more than 140 training institutions in Tanzania, about 20 of which are higher education training institutions. Teaching and learning in these institutions are guided by the Higher Education Training Policy of 1995. Some of the goals of the policy are to encourage equitable distribution of education institutions and resources, expand and improve girls' education and enable gifted and disabled children to access appropriate education and training. Developing programs to ensure access to education for disadvantaged groups was among the chief objectives of the policy. Unfortunately, however, the obligations and commitments of the state and the community were not clearly delineated in the policy.

According to Castro and Levy (2001), there are four main functions of higher education. First, higher education is meant in general to develop analytical skills that are useful in any occupation or activity. Second, it should enable specialised professional development. This refers to preparing students for specific jobs requiring extensive formal education. Our higher learning institutions are not doing well at either of these first two functions. Most of our curricula is not geared towards enabling members of the community to solve their problems. Moreover the curricular contents in our learning institutions do not correspond directly to the jobs available out there. This leads to underemployment and failure to deliver by our graduates. To make matters worse, we are not doing enough in providing career guidance and counselling to our students.

The third main function of higher education, according to Castro and Levy (2001), is technological training and development. In this regard, our higher learning institutions are lagging further and further behind. They lack equipment, and the available equipment is often outdated or lacking qualified members of staff to operate or maintain it. Funds set aside for purchase and maintenance of equipment are seriously inadequate.

Finally, according to Castro and Levy (2001), there is the issue of "academic leadership", the most prestigious function of higher education. They contend that academic leadership requires sophisticated original research published in rigorously reviewed, internationally recognised outlets. However, this cannot happen without adequate funding for research, and it is the obligation of the state to see to it that the academic community gets research funds. One would certainly be curious to find out the amount of original research conducted and published by our members of staff and students in both local and international journals. One would also want to know the impact of the research on the community and state. It is important that research findings are consumed by the community and used to solve problems rather than ending up in shelves as decorations or signs of achievement or for promotions. However, due to lack of journals and other resources, most of our members of staff do not get to publish their research and end up keeping their ideas to themselves. Also some of their research does not address the real community issues. It is fair to conclude that members of the community do not get to share, discuss and enjoy the fruits of most of our research. What then is our obligation to the state and community?

State and Community Commitment in Higher Education

The commitment of the state and the community in higher education is insufficient. Both the state and the community have failed to fund higher education institutions adequately. This is evidenced by the budget set aside for higher education. For example in the past 5 years the budget has been dwindling, as Table 1 indicates. We also do not know how much our communities contribute in cash or kind.

Table 1: University of Dar es Salaam Budget Proposal and Approved Budget for 1999/2000 – 2003/2004

Year	UDSM Proposal	Government Approval	UDSM vs Govt Budget (%)
1999/2000	35,052,826,003	15,658,204,000	56
2000/2001	28,010,713,125	19,454,915,306	69
2001/2002	23,950,500,000	12,962,933,600	54
2002/2003	24,115,444,308	14,413,011,824	60
2003/2004	29,442,119,506	16,869,293,885	57

Source: University of Dar es Salaam (2004) Five-Year Strategic Plan

Table 1 clearly indicates that, whereas the University of Dar es Salaam prepares a budget proposal according to her needs, the institution always re-
ceives much less than requested. With such a trend how do we realise the
functions of higher education? Where are the various communities in Tanzania? Can they not step in and assist? There are institutions and members of
various communities sponsoring a variety of activities. We have some even
sponsoring beauty contests, dances, and so on. Could such money not be
used in higher education? How serious are members of the community in
providing higher education? It is well understood that communities feel that
it is the role of the state to provide education. However the time has come
for members of the community to step in and play their part in higher education. Higher education should not be a ball to be bounced forth and back by
various teams who will never score a single goal. Let there be concerted efforts.

It is also interesting to observe that there are more funds available for
higher education from donors than from the government, as indicated in
Table 2. NORAD, SIDA/SAREC, WHO, VLIR, NUFU, Carnegie and other
donors have contributed more to higher education than our own communities
and even our own government. It is high time that the state and community place
a higher value on education and get more involved. We must own our own
education!

Table 2: Strategic Support to the University of Dar es Salaam,
1998/99 to 2002/2003

Source	2000/2001	2001/2002	2002/2003
Donors	15,134,016.00	14,601,845.00	15,171,591.00
Tanzanian Government	11,610,607.90	9,972,656.00	11,175,822.00

Source: University of Dar es Salaam (2004) Five-Year Strategic Plan

It should be borne in mind that the state and communities are obliged to
provide education to their citizens and members, who are legally recognised
men and women belonging to the state or community they live in. They have
the right to require education services (perfect type obligation) or to receive
education in the form of charity or as a mere duty (imperfect obligation). It is
evident that there are very few communities that sponsor students for higher
education. Most of these are religious organisations, with Christian ones leading
the way. The rest is left to the government, whose hands cannot stretch very
far bearing in mind, its many other commitments. While I agree that higher
education should be considered a perfect obligation, the state also has to be

accountable and liable for the education of Tanzanians, including those with disabilities, members of minority groups and those from disadvantaged regions. After all they are citizens of this nation and taxpayers. At the same time members of the community must contribute to higher education. They will benefit from the education and, in reciprocation, assist in nation building. It is a give-and-take exercise.

It should also be noted that the education of all citizens is of vital importance to the state's well-being. Higher education should therefore not be considered a rare commodity or be left to the market to determine the demand and supply. Higher Education should not be a commercial product. It is a social good, and both the state and members of the community have to share the responsibility for providing education to our sons and daughters. Members of the community should own the process in higher education, take charge and control the education provided to all citizens. The state and the community have to fulfill their obligation to provide higher education and must be committed to set professional standards in research, consultancy and community service in higher learning institutions. Standards have to be maintained with benchmarks that will assist in maintaining the quality of higher education and of knowledge creation. Meanwhile, the contribution of academicians and researchers, as well as other members of the higher education community, is also essential. The university should continue to cherish divergent thinking and diversity of ideas as a way of facilitating creativity in higher education and innovation for national development, and the community must be involved in decision-making on crucial issues in higher-education institutions.

The community has a moral obligation to see to it that:

- higher-education institutions have competent, fully qualified faculty members

- adequate higher-education opportunities and programmes are available for special-needs students, including gifted and talented students

- appropriate academic standards are maintained

- policies are in place that hold individuals, schools and colleges accountable for higher education

- local governments and local communities are organised and responsible in enhancing higher education.

For its part, the state has an obligation to:

- ensure there are adequate fiscal resources to guarantee high-quality education

- provide adequate and appropriate technology and infrastructure for all students, including those with special needs

- develop and maintain a cohesive system of first-rate higher-learning institutions that prepare students well for the world of work.

The Task Ahead

Let us make sure that we invest strongly in higher education so that we benefit from a highly educated population. Local governments, the central government and members of the community all have to be involved in subsidising higher-education costs. In particular the contribution of the community and the state in higher education must be improved, sought for and appreciated. My observations have clearly indicated that the state and community have not invested enough in higher education. It can therefore be concluded that the time has come for the community to take charge as follows:

- Tanzania as a community has to recognise the need and rationale for promoting higher education through self-determination and self-organisation.

- High-school students must be encouraged to pursue more specialised and technical professions.

- The quality of education must be improved and maintained so that students have access to quality instruction.

- The government and community authorities should place the funding of higher education further up on their agendas.

- There is need for investing in community media in order to promote a wider discussion of issues concerning higher education.

- There is need to share common resources and facilities between local governments and NGOs.

- The various religious organisations in the country must be continuously encouraged and assisted as partners with the government to invest in higher education.

References

Castro, C. de Maura and Levy, D. C., 2001, *Four Functions of Higher Education*, Boston: Centre for International Higher Education.

Ishumi, A. G., 2000, *Access to and Equity in Education in Tanzania*, Unpublished manuscript.

Possi, M. K., 2003, *Low Representation of Disadvantaged Groups in Higher Education Institutions*, Paper presented for a workshop on 27 March 2003 in Higher Education Office, Dar es Salaam, Tanzania.

Appendices

Proceedings of the Conference on Academic Freedom and Social Responsibility

Whitesands Hotel, Dar Es Salaam, 11-12 February 2005

DAY ONE: 10/02/05

Welcoming Professor Mmari

The Vice-Chair UDASA, Professor Saida Yahya-Othman, welcomed Professor Mmari, the current Vice-Chancellor of Open University. She cited the 1990 Dar es Salaam Declaration as a milestone in academic freedom in Africa. She noted that CODESRIA had financed the workshop leading to the declaration and that it was the same Dakar-based council for research in Africa which is responsible for this workshop. She commended UDASA for charting the way forward for academic freedom in the region. She recognised the previous chairs of UDASA and expressed how proud UDASA is to have Professor Mmari deliver the keynote address, as he had been the first chairperson of the academic staff organisation, started during a momentous and crisis-ridden period. She praised Professor Mmari as a dynamic scholar eager to foster academic freedom and excellence as well as the welfare of fellow academicians.

Professor Mmari's Keynote Address – 'Glimpses of Nationalist Academics'

Professor Mmari gave a historical background to the growth of university education in East Africa, from the colonial days to the current period in which private universities are mushrooming and the commercialisation of university education has become the order of the day. He lauded UDASA's struggle to maintain the cardinal principle of university education, which is academic freedom. He pointed out that UDASA has stood the test of time since it produced the Dar es Salaam Declaration, and stressed that academic freedom grows out of the struggle for freedom of thought and expression, a basic human right in any free society. Professor Mmari recounted the history of academic freedom since the birth of universities and observed that academic freedom is secure whenever the prestige of university education is high, but insecure when universities do not have such prestige. He described the growth of the university system in East Africa as it grappled with nationalist, political, ideological, economic and global ramifications. He concluded his presentation by showing how factors such as the recent mass expansion of university intakes, the introduction of private providers and the influence of political agendas impact adversely on university education, especially on academic freedom and the maintenance of high academic standards. In conclusion, he called for a return to an environment which will 'allow universities the freedom to do their work as best they know how .'

Vote of Thanks

In thanking Professor Mmari, the UDASA chairperson, Professor Chachage, extolled him as a staunch and unflinching supporter of academic freedom in the various positions he has held and as a pioneer of honest, dynamic leadership in his role as the first UDASA chairperson.

Discussion

The discussion which followed described Professor Mmari as a dedicated public servant and a true academician who has sacrificed a lot in pursuit of knowledge, excellence and fairness. A question was posed: why do many activists abdicate or give up their militancy once they get better or higher jobs. Professor Mmari explained that very few people practice in earnest what they preach and thus the attainment even of deanships and department headship led some people to forsake their Professoressional stance. Another point raised was the fate of academic freedom in light of market forces dictating policies to academia, restricting academic freedom and watering down academic standards. Professor Mmari responded that there is a need to return to the original role of universities to ward off hijacking by politicians. Another participant inquired whether the original philosophy of the universities was still practicable or relevant in a globalised world. The state of current university was questioned, and it was pointed out that other forces were taking over at the expense of academic freedom. Consequently excellence suffers, as education has been watered down and standards are falling continuously.

Professor Kanywanyi on 'Academic Freedom, Autonomy of Institutions of Higher Learning and Social Responsibility of Academicians'

Professor Kanywanyi introduced his presentation by noting how huge and heavily loaded topic it was. The aim of his paper, he said, was to review the original Dar es Salaam Declaration, discuss how far it had been implemented and attempt a critique of the declaration itself. He posed some intriguing questions, while pointing out that although the declaration clearly enunciated the principles of academic freedom, it offered no practical programme for the implementation of the principles. As a result, the declaration, in his view, left the issue of academic freedom hanging in mid-air, with no legs to stand on, heads to carry it forward or hands to guide it along a charted path. This, he contended, was a critical omission that raised questions about the legitimacy of the declaration. He asked: how can a declaration with 'shall' provisions be enforced? Can it be self-executing?

On academic freedom, Professor Kanywanyi made a number of critical remarks. He pointed out that there has been no jurisprudential discourse on the issues raised by the Dar es Salaam Declaration except one paper by Professor Issa Shivji. He contended in particular with Article 25 of the declaration on 'fear and victimisation', wondered who is being addressed here and recommended that the article be deleted. He went on to deal with the issues of autonomy and social responsibility and concluded by saying that his main aim had been to stimulate further discussion on the declaration.

Discussion

The discussion of Professor Kanywanyi's paper centred on the need to design and operationalise the provisions of the Dar es Salaam Declaration by providing tools for their implementation. However, some discussants argued that the declaration was not a legal document but a political statement meant to raise awareness on the rights and obligations of academics and should be evaluated from this perspective. It was explained that in many ways the declaration had been useful. For example, the events which followed the declaration, such as the removal of the then VC, student unrest and the fate of some members of the academic staff, were influenced in one way or another by declaration. In hindsight, indeed, some critical aspects were overlooked then. Participants were reminded that the Dar es Salaam Declaration was adopted by six institutions which are now either fully fledged universities or colleges. The expectation then was that each institution would take the initiative to implement the declaration. It was agreed that some mechanisms for implementation, such as legal provisions, were needed. On the whole, it was agreed that Professor Kanywanyi's critique raised interesting issues and showed the need to revisit the 1990 document in the 2005 setting.

Professor Chachage on 'The University as a Site of Knowledge: The Role of Basic Research'

Professor Chachage cited the April 2003 confrontation between UDASA and the university administration on the proposed visit of the USA Ambassador to UDSM, which raised a number of questions about national independence and the implications of offending the providers of aid to universities and the like. He posed a number of questions relating to academic freedom and independent research: How can a university be a site of knowledge if it has to fear offending the powers-that-be? How can basic research be conducted when donors and international financial institutions dominate academia? Professor Chachage contended that there is no academic freedom in abstract and appraised the 1990 and 1991 declarations in the context of a crisis-ridden region undergoing structural adjustment programmes (SAPs). He noted that the declarations were not explicit on the issue of universities as sites of knowledge and dwelt much on the contribution by the French writer Lyotard on the changing nature of knowledge in capitalist countries and the role of universities in the postmodern age. He then dealt with neo-liberalism and institutional transformations in Tanzania and the role of World Bank and IMF in shaping primary, tertiary and vocational education. He lamented how higher education had been drawn into the world market and made into a commodity, observing that 'academic freedom belongs to those who control and own the means of production of knowledge and its dissemination and not those who generate [knowledge]'.

Professor Chachage discussed how basic research has suffered in the light of consultancies, a preoccupation of many academicians who excel at academic 'entrepreneurship'. He concluded that, because education is geared towards the market, many students and even teachers only read from utilitarian motives such as passing examinations or getting promoted. In conclusion, he argued for the need to go back to the noble role of the university as a creator and disseminator of knowledge.

Discussion

It was agreed that universities are supposed to be about knowledge production, but that the challenge is to capture the magnitude of the problem and the extent to which universities have departed from their original role. The question is: do we have social responsibility or should we continue to accept being driven by politicians? The problem of the commercialisation of higher education was discussed at length, as well as the corruption in many facets of life which had implications also for the education sector. It was noted that universities were dying with the introduction of market-oriented programmes.

Professor Mhina on 'Implications of Privatisation and Marketisation of Higher Education for the Generation of Knowledge and Social Transformation'

Professor Mhina apportioned blame for the crisis of higher education squarely on the World Bank, adding that in Tanzania, the crisis was compounded by economic problems and governance issues. He alluded to the situation at UDSM and its problems with staffing, equipment and space as a direct result of the privatisation and marketisation of higher education. He noted that government was reducing its spending on higher education while at the same time forcing a rampant expansion in enrollment rates not matched by infrastructural and human resources. He also raised issues about equity and access to higher education. He touched on the generation and recycling of knowledge and singled out consultancies as being responsible for the decline in the production of new knowledge. In conclusion, Professor Mhina conceded that the demand for higher education is overwhelming and that there is a need therefore, for more universities (even private ones). However, he argued strongly that the state has to live up to its obligation to be the main provider of higher education to its citizens.

Discussion

The discussion dwelt on the fact that administrators and politicians insist on increasing the intake of students into higher learning institutions, but they do not realise the ramifications of such growth. It was noted that the commercialisation of higher education seems to be here to stay and that academicians seem unable to prevent or control it, as popular programmes, tailor-made to fit even in-service staff, are in vogue in the region. At the same time, it was noted that the quality of higher education has suffered. It was pointed out that Northern universities trade on education by designing programmes which attract students from the developing world, but which could very well be taught in their countries of origin. Participants remembered with nostalgia the lively ideological classes of the 1970s at the University of Dar es Salaam and compared them to today's lethargic situation where one is lucky to attract a handful of attendants to a seminar presentation. Participants were urged to compare the current Tanzanian situation with that of other countries such as Cuba, where the state has invested so heavily in education that 30 percent of its citizens are in school, and for free at that. It was concluded that university problems reflected larger societal problems, and that these are the problems that lead to the marginalisation, privatisation and marketisation of higher education.

Professor Possi on 'The Obligations of the State and Communities in the Provision of Higher Education'

Professor Possi argued that higher education is now at a cross roads and needs to be rescued, an outcry heard from many quarters. The deterioration of the quality of education was mentioned by many concerned citizens who listed reasons such as inadequate teaching staff, materials, space and facilities. She also cited the problem of minority groups being forgotten. Defining education as the quest for learning, she argued for the obligation of the state and the community at large to provide education for their citizens. Professor Possi pointed out that the provision of education is multi-faceted and that in Tanzania higher education is guided by a 1995 policy which is intended to promote equity but does not clearly delineate the obligations of the state and the community. She lamented that both the state and the community have failed to fund higher education adequately, leaving it to donors to come in and help. Referring to various countries in the North which have made great strides in higher education, she urged Tanzania to learn from them. The task ahead, Professor Possi argued, is to ensure greater investment in higher education by every sector of the country, including local government, local communities and even NGOs.

Discussion

Participants concurred on the necessity of the state and other stakeholders to live up to their obligations. It was observed that the paramount role of the state in providing education to its people is stated as a right in the original constitution, whereas now the constitution reads that a person has a duty of self-education.

Dr Cardoso on 'The State of Universities and Academic Freedom in Africa'

Dr Cardoso called for a new concept of the university in Africa. He explained how CODESRIA strives to reinforce and foster academic freedom and help African universities to do their work properly. For example, he cited how post-graduate studies suffer from meagre financial resources and lack of mentoring and explained how CODESRIA tries hard to come to grips with this predicament by sponsoring workshops throughout sub-Saharan Africa. CODESRIA, he said, has identified the needs of academicians and universities in Africa and is doing its best to help. He noted that the Dar es Salaam

Declaration originated during momentous and crisis-ridden times but that, despite this, it was full of hope. This may seem paradoxical, he observed, yet the past fourteen years have shown how academics can fight for their freedoms and for the integrity of the university as an arena for generating and disseminating knowledge.

DAY TWO: 11/02/05

Experiences from Various Universities

UDASA Experience (Dr Yared Kihore)

Dr Kihore's presentation treated three sub-themes. The first sub-theme was the historical background of UDASA and its fight for academic freedom. The presenter pointed out that UDASA has fought for academic freedom since its inception, for example, by campaigning for the election of Deans of Faculties and Heads of Departments. Dr Kihore's second sub-theme concerned the state of academic programmes. He explained that the problems with academic programmes ranged from shortage of staff to increasing number of students, from inadequate facilities to problems associated with semesterisation. All these are yet to be solved, but some require urgent and immediate attention. Dr Kihore reiterated that, despite all these problems at the UDSM, UDASA is committed to uphold and spearhead the struggle for high academic standards. The third sub-theme was social responsibility. Dr Kihore observed that from the beginning UDASA has participated in a lot of highly visible activities, illustrating its sense of responsibility towards Tanzanian society. For example, UDASA followed up on the Kilombero massacres of 1986, when its members visited the scene, although they were blocked by the powers-that-be. Nevertheless UDASA made its point through various statements, which had some impact on the way things were conducted after the Kilombero incidents. He observed that UDASA was also at the forefront in many other protests and has taken a stand, not only on the way UDSM is administered, but also on government highhandedness and even on international issues. He concluded that there is no way UDASA can avoid playing its assertive role in society and that this workshop was a continuation of that effort.

SUASA Experience (Professor Kambarage)

The presentation on Sokoine University of Agriculture Academic Staff Association (SUASA) was read by Professor K. D. Kambarage. He began with a brief history of Sokoine University of Agriculture (SUA) and then mentioned the main constraints facing SUASA:

1. No government mechanism to tap the human resources of the university

2. Lack of partnership between academicians and government ministries

3. Inadequate forums for sharing and exchanging ideas

4. Lack of transparency and confidentiality in discussing staff issues

5. Lack of consensus on the question of collective responsibility, that is, the policy that once a decision has been made, all members must abide by it

6. The constraining effect on academic freedom of some academic staff occupying administrative positions

7. Lack of confidence of academicians to express their ideas.

8. Poor motivation among staff due to poor remuneration, lack of research funding and career development opportunities and the ongoing "brain drain".

Dr Kambarage argued for five key ways to address these problems:

1. Focus on improving the working environment, especially with regard to facilities, training, office space and equipment

2. Forge partnerships to push for higher pay packages and improved pension schemes

3. Insist on recognising and respecting local expertise.

4. Call for good governance at all levels of university administration

5. Devise mechanisms to sensitise university staff on the Dar es Salaam Declaration.

State University of Zanzibar (Mr Salim Hamad)

Mr Hamad observed that it is now three years since the inception of the State University of Zanzibar (SUZA) and it still does not have a full-fledged academic staff association, but only an interim committee. He reported that the interim committee had drafted a constitution, which came out in October 2004, and has managed to bring the issues of salary scales and leave allowances to the attention of the university administration. He highlighted some of the main problems facing members of staff at SUZA as:

- Directors instead of academicians conducting interviews for new members of academic staff

- Academic staff having to teach courses outside their specialisations

- The administration communicating only verbally with the interim committee

- Appointment of Deans, Directors and Heads of Departments remaining in the hands of the Vice-Chancellor

- Lack of research units.

IFM-Academic Staff Assembly (Mr C. D. N. Kassala)

Mr Kassala gave a brief background of IFM and pointed out that the IFM Academic Staff Assembly (IFMASA) is an autonomous association registered by the Ministry of Home Affairs. He reported that IFMASA tried to work with local trade union RAAWU in an attempt to improve the educational levels of auxiliary staff working with IFM, but that management intervened and stopped this initiative. Other efforts by IFMASA have mainly been directed at improving salary scales, advocating for the election of heads of departments, orienting new members of staff and establishing a research and publication department. However they have had little success due to:

1. Inadequate facilities such as computer equipment and office space.

2. The increasing tendency of students to demand a say in the management's choice of lecturers, the level of material and content to be taught and the number of assignments.

Zanzibar University (Mr Lubowa Luwalira)

Mr Luwalira began with a brief background of Zanzibar National University (ZANU) and pointed out that academic staff at ZANU have very similar problems to those of their colleagues at SUZA. He observed that academic staff have no say on the choice and number of courses to be taught and that there is no program for staff development. He reported that the university lacks computerised library facilities and also observed that students lacked a reading culture.

Moshi University College Academic Staff Association (Mr Eligius Banjamin Danda)

Mr Danda provided a brief background of the Moshi University College of Co-operative and Business Studies (MUCCOBS), which came into being by upgrading the former Co-operative College Moshi into a constituent college of Sokoine University of Agriculture (SUA). MUCCOBS is established under Declaration Order No. 22 of 2004, which recognises the academic association as a participatory organ of the college. There is a specific section in the Declaration Order on the representation of the academic staff association on faculty boards and on the Governing Board of the college. Mr Danda observed that the process of successful transformation owes much to a consultative process between the academic staff and management. In other words, the academic association championed the process of transforming from a mere institute to a constituent college of SUA. He reported that academic staff also control the process for election of academic heads of departments, faculty deans and directors at the college.

Arisa (Dr Mtalo)

Dr Mtalo began by relating how the former Ardhi Institute was transformed into the University College of Land and Architectural Studies (UCLAS) of the UDSM in 1996. On academic freedom, he said that the ability of academic staff to have an important say on matters relating to development of the constituent college varied with changes of leadership (principals). Thus, there is a lot of confusion at UCLAS, largely because of the inappropriate environment ushered in by the current leadership. Dr Mtalo observed that the situation at UCLAS is strange, as it is students who have proved more effective in demanding and protecting their academic freedoms. He concluded by pointing out that that academic staff receive low salaries and are not sure of their pension schemes.

Kenyan Universities Academic Staff Union (Mr John H. Nderitu)

Mr Nderitu opened by expressing his gratitude to the organisers of the workshop for having invited the Kenyan Universities Academic Staff Union (UASU), saying that this noble gesture will go a long way in consolidating the relationship between UASU and other associations participating in the workshop. He reported that UASU has been registered in May 2003 as a union. It now has at least a secretariat in all the Kenyan public universities and last year it led its members in an industrial action which lasted for three months in seven public universities. He thanked UDSM staff for faxing their salary structures for reference by their Kenyan counterparts and observed that UASU has enhanced interaction of academicians within and amongst universities and is thereby promoting academic freedom. The Deputy Secretary of UASU, Muga K'olale, added that the only reason UASU succeeded was unity, saying that in the past academic staff lacked a structure to fight for academic freedom. He argued that, in the past, universities had been treated as obstacles to development and perceived by the state as sources of sedition. He added that Kenyans were completely ignorant of what university lecturers earned and concluded by saying that the union is now making efforts to convince the wider society that its struggles go beyond the stomach! For example, it is determined to investigate and help root out corruption in the public universities.

Makerere University Academic Staff Association (Mr T. E. Mishambi)

Like previous presentations, this began with a brief background of Makerere University and the Makerere University Academic Staff Association (MUASA) and went on to explain the circumstances surrounding the appointment of the Makerere University Vice-Chancellor, MUASA's intervention and the issues of academic freedom this raised. The second part of the presentation dwelt on the issue of commercialisation of education. Mr Mishambi explained how the Uganda government had enticed universities to come up with market-driven programs so as to attract more private sponsorship students and observed that some faculty members benefit from the money paid by private students in the form of so-called top-up allowances.

Discussion

Professor Shivji observed that some of the gains made by UDASA have actually been reversed and never defended, citing the elections of deans and heads of departments as glaring examples. He recommended that, in order to ensure that academic staff do not become socially irrelevant, they should not fight for selfish and individual benefits but rather for larger social causes. Professor Shivji observed that the transformation of universities has had very little input from academicians and complained of the prevalence of not only contract labour but even casual labour in private universities. This situation is eroding security of tenure. Professor Shivji decried the apathy of some members of academic associations, noting that this attitude weakens the associations.

Professor Othman called attention to the mushrooming of staff associations and said he was struck in particular by the presentation from Zanzibar University. He urged the presenter and his colleagues to continue their struggle to have their own staff association.

Professor Chachage pointed out that discussions were held some years ago between SUASA and UDASA on the possibility of forming a trade union for university staff. It had been agreed in principle to establish a union while retaining UDASA. He further noted that engineering, science and medicine courses can hardly be found in private universities. He said that offering these essential courses underlines the importance of public universities.

Professor Yahya-Othman noted the apathy and lack of vitality in academic staff associations. She observed that some of the causal factors are of the members' own making, as observed by Professor Kanywanyi in his earlier presentation. She accordingly asked UDASA to give its members guidance on how to act in solidarity with positions taken by the association. Professor M. Baregu then observed that the Kenyan experience marks a bolder attempt to establish academic freedom, recommending that UDASA can borrow from the Kenyan model. Mr S. Hamad added that there is a need not only to form national and regional associations but also a continent-wide umbrella association.

Dr Muga K'olale stressed that the professional element should be emphasised in any notion of academic labour unionisation, while Dr Mtalo called for an increase in the number of universities rather than a focus on increasing the numbers of students in the few existing ones. He recommended that academic associations should have a firmer say on matters of quality of education and decried "rumour-mongering and gossiping" within universities.

Reviving East African Social Science Discourse and Discussion on Formation of Umbrella Association (Professor I. G. Shivji)

In his presentation, Professor Shivji started with a brief background on the academic debates of the 1960s and 1970s. In a nutshell, he said that in those days, 'no East African or African event passed without there being a discussion and surgical analysis of whether it was in the interest of the people or of the petty bourgeoisie and/or imperialism'. Professor Shivji then reviewed the state of interaction between the universities in East Africa as far as intellectual debate is concerned. He went back to the vibrant academic debates on university campuses of the 1960s and 1970s for inspiration in grappling with the existing intellectual inertia and apparent marketisation of academia, a direct result of the invasion of neo-liberal agenda. In the end he proposesd some mechanisms for an eastern African Discourse. As background Professor Shivji sketched the political climate since nationalist days through military coups into the adoption of different development agendas in the East African countries. He lauded the radical discourses that had characterised academia, especially at the University of Dar es Salaam with its animated ideological classes, publications and nurturing of prospective leaders of the region. However, due to adverse political developments such as the coup in Uganda, the Uganda-Tanzania war and the collapse of the East African Community, academia was affected to the detriment of coherent discourse. The intellectual and academic climate in the three countries declined as neo-liberal policies took hold through structural adjustment programmes and the commercialisation of higher education. Today, according to Professor Shivji, there is no intellectual discourse, which ought to be the lifeline of any university community. He urged participants to reinvent an East African discourse, this time rooted in genuine pan-Africanism. To this end Professor Shivji proposed the formation of a forum as a mechanism to bring together East African intellectuals as a way of adhering to the Dar es Salaam and Kampala declarations, which obliged us to shoulder our social responsibility, that is, 'to discourse and expose the ills of society'. By 'East African', Professor Shivji explained, he meant Rwanda, Burundi and DRC in addition to Kenya, Uganda and Tanzania. He concluded his presentation by calling for the revival of the previously rotating East African Social Sciences Conference under the aegis and initiative of our staff associations.

Discussion

There was unanimous support for the establishment of an umbrella association, as there are so many benefits to be gained. UDASA was ready to take the initiative of organising a meeting of associations' leaders to develop a plan for the way forward. It was explained that three associations, UDASA, ARISA and SUASA, had already come up with the name TUASA for the proposed Tanzanian union of academic organisations and even drawn up a constitution for the same. It was further revealed that there were provisions for other associations to join TUASA. It was agreed that the Kenyan team should lead the way in organising an East African academic umbrella body. It was agreed that the Eastern Africa Social Sciences Conference should be revived and, if possible, a conference should be convened this year. The matter was left for UDASA's Academic Affairs Committee to handle. It was agreed that the workshop should come out with a communiqué discussing the state of academia in the region and reflecting the deliberations of the workshop.

Closing

The workshop was closed at 19.10 hrs by the Chairman of UDASA, Professor Chachage. He thanked all participants for their valuable and engaging contributions. He also paid tribute to CODESRIA for extending its assistance in organising the workshop. Professor Chachage reminded participants of the role played by CODESRIA in organising an earlier forum in 1990 which led to the Dar es Salaam Declaration. He specifically thanked Dr Carlos Cardoso of CODESRIA for facilitating this workshop, as well as members of the Coordinating Committee, specifically Professor I.G. Shivji, Dr M. Bakari, Professor Saida Yahya-Othman and Dr N. Kamata.

Observations

Academic Freedom

1. The increasingly top-down approach to curriculum development, i.e., modularisation and semesterisation, has had a negative effect on the content and quality of education.

2. The contribution of the universities to the development of what should be taught in primary and secondary schools has been eroded.

3. The separation of higher education and primary/secondary education into two separate ministries has had a negative impact on the development of education in Tanzania. It has also led to a neglect of learners' needs, especially when they join the universities.

4. Donor dependency by universities has affected the content of education and constrained the freedom of choice of what should be taught and the type of books and other resources.

5. Limited funding for universities is a major constraint and leads to donor dependency.

6. Limited/meagre funding both by government and donors has caused universities to struggle to stand on their own and has resulted in rushing to succumb to the so-called market driven degree programmes and the commercialisation of university services.

7. The commercialisation of university programmes has led to the government abdicating its role to provide for higher education and left this to students and their parents. The state has an obligation to provide education to its citizens as a right.

8. The loans scheme in Tanzania curtails academic freedom and has become an excuse for government to run away from its responsibility to provide for higher education.

9. The issue of conditions for loans and the need for collateral will disadvantage children from poor families.

10. The loans scheme also affects the right of students to freely choose the degree programmes they want to pursue.

11. The World Bank and IMF conditions for financial assistance for developing countries have favoured funding for primary and secondary education at the expense of university education.

12. The quality of students joining the universities has deteriorated. Most of those who join have been taught to pass examinations and not to acquire knowledge. This has also affected the quality of university graduates.

13. The disparity between the secondary education system in Kenya and that in Tanzania and Uganda has affected the mobility of students within the region.

14. The reading culture is poor, and this affects the imparting and transmission of knowledge. This is a result of lack of books in primary and secondary schools

15. The tuition syndrome in primary and secondary schools is also affecting the quality of training and of the graduates.

16. Mass enrollment without matching resources has seriously affected the quality of higher education.

17. Poor conditions of service (salaries, pensions, medical, insurance, housing and opportunities for staff development) have contributed to low morale and lack of commitment among academics.

18. The policies on staff development and training are haphazard, and universities lack adequate resources to implement them.

19. Consultancies and commercial "research" have overridden the responsibility to create and impart knowledge and have contributed to apathy in the academic vocation, watered-down academic freedom and low participation in national debates on pertinent issues that affect society.

20. Academics' response to commercialisation of programmes affects the quality of education and academic freedom and compromises standards so as to attract more private students

Creation and Dissemination of Knowledge

1. Inadequate government funding invites donor-driven research which may be irrelevant to our countries.

2. Lack of government funding for research, publication, outreach programmes, sabbatical leaves and participation in workshops and conferences has reduced our academics to beggars and servants of the donors that sponsor them.

3. Privatisation of research and consultancy at the expense of teaching is eroding the primary mission of the university to generate and transmit knowledge.

4. Lack of mechanisms or funds to enable academics to prepare compendia and source books for use in the universities severely limits both research and teaching.

Infrastucture

1. Library spaces and resources do not match the expanded enrollment of students. Libraries are poorly funded and are not given the required priority. They are dependent on donors. Equipping and networking libraries properly is essential to enhance resource-sharing and fuller utilisation.

2. Lecture rooms, laboratories and equipment also do not match the increasing enrollment.

3. Academics are not provided with adequate facilities (offices, computers, books, etc.) to perform their work efficiently.

University Governance

1. There is a notably top-down, bureaucratic approach to the running of universities. This erodes participatory decision-making within academic units and the university community generally.

2. The practice of appointing heads of departments and deans of faculties by higher authorities reinforces the top-down management approach. Heads and deans should be elected by their academic colleagues and peers instead of being appointed.

3. The tendency for academics to be appointed as managers in university administrations is eroding collegiality.

Resolution on Academic Freedom and the Social Responsibilities of Academics adopted by the Academic Staff Associations of East Africa on 11 February 2005

The State of the Academy

We, the representatives of the East African academic staff associations, having deliberated on the state of the universities in our respective countries, have noted with concern that the role of universities as sites for the production and transmission of knowledge has been eroded over the years, particularly with the advent of neo-liberal economic and political policies.

We note that there is excessive interference by non-professional administrators, consultants and advisors in the determination of forms of knowledge, how knowledge is produced and imparted and methods of research. We have been witnessing the increasing withdrawal of our respective governments from funding of public universities, leaving this responsibility to international financial institutions (IFIs) and donors. This has resulted in undue interference by these agencies in our institutions. The wholesale adoption of the market ideology by the management of our universities, through the so-called institutional transformation programmes, has diluted the coherence, social relevance and depth of the courses taught and the kind of research that is prioritised and supported.

We have further noted that the enforced expansion of student enrollments without a corresponding development of human and material resources, along with the bureaucratisation of the universities, have negatively impacted on the quality of knowledge production and transmission to the detriment of the long term goals of our countries.

We have recalled the *Dar es Salaam Declaration on Academic Freedom and Social Responsibility of Academics* of 1990 and *The Kampala Declaration on Intellectual*

Freedom and Social Responsibility of 1991 and have reaffirmed our commitment to uphold the academic freedoms stated in the two declarations. We have also solemnly rededicated ourselves to undertake our social responsibility to serve our communities. We have again underlined the need for our governments to take seriously their duty to guarantee equal and equitable education for their people, making available an adequate proportion of their national incomes for education and guaranteeing their academics the right to determine what is taught and how it is taught without compromising the interests of the people.

We reject the externally induced institutional transformations which are reducing our institutions of higher learning to glorified high schools or poly-technics, and we reject the view that the staff and students of universities are mere beneficiaries rather than the real actors in the processes of production and transmission of knowledge.

We have therefore resolved to form national and regional organisations to promote and defend knowledge and fight for better working conditions for both academic staff and students in our institutions of higher learning.

We believe that our young generation and our people as a whole are entitled to wholesome knowledge and have a right to think for themselves as part of the fundamental right of self-determination that our nationalist leaders fought for.

Name of Representative	Name of Association	Name of Institution	Signature
Mr Eligius Benjamin Danda	MUCASA (Moshi University College Academic Staff Association)	Moshi University of Cooperative and Business Studies, Tanzania	[signed]
Dr Elifuraha G. Mtalo	ARISA (UCLAS Academic Staff Assembly) Tanzania	University College of Lands and Architectural Studies (UCLAS),	[signed]
Mr Salim Othman Hamad	SUZAASA (The State University of Zanzibar Academic Staff Association)	The State University of Zanzibar (SUZA), Tanzania	[signed]
Prof. Chachage S. L. Chachage	UDASA (University of Dar es Salaam Academic Staff Assembly)	University of Dar es Salaam, Tanzania	[signed]
Prof. John H. Nderutu	UASU (University Academic Staff Union)	University of Nairobi, Kenya	[signed]
Mr Musaha Esebe	UASU (University Academic Staff Union)	Moi University, Kenya	[signed]
Mr Muga K'olale	UASU (University Academic Staff Union)	Egerton University, Kenya	[signed]
Dr Ezra M. Twesigomwe	MUASA (Makerere University Staff Association)	Makerere University, Uganda	[signed]
Mr Lubowa Luwalira	Zanzibar University Staff Academic Assembly	Zanzibar University, Zanzibar	[signed]
Prof. D. M. Kambarage	SUASA (Sokoine University Academic Staff Assembly)	Sokoine University of Agriculture, Tanzania	[signed]

The Kampala Declaration on Intellectual Freedom and Social Responsibility
November 1990

Preamble

Intellectual freedom in Africa is currently threatened; to an unprecedented degree. The historically produced and persistent economic, political and social crisis of our continent continues to undermine development in all spheres. The imposition of unpopular structural adjustment programmes has been accompanied by increased political repression, widespread poverty and intense human suffering.

African people are responding to these intolerable conditions by intensifying their struggles for democracy and human rights. The struggle for intellectual freedom is an integral part of the struggle of our people for human rights. Just as popular forces are waging a struggle for democracy and human rights, so are African academics, intellectuals, students and other members of the intelligentsia deeply involved in their own struggles for intellectual and academic freedom.

Aware that the African states are parties to international and regional human rights instruments, including the African Charter for Human and People's rights, and convinced that we, the African intellectual community, have an obligation both to fight for our rights as well as to raise the rights consciousness of our people, we mat in Kampala to reaffirm our commitment to the Charter, set normal standards to guide the exercise of intellectual freedom and remind ourselves of our social responsibility as intellectuals.

We have thus adopted the Kampala Declaration on Intellectual Freedom and Social Responsibility on this 29th day of November, 1990.

May the Declaration be a standard-bearer for the African intellectual community to assert its autonomy and undertake its responsibility to the people of our continent.

Chapter I: Fundamental Rights and Freedoms

Section A: Intellectual Rights and Freedoms

Article 1

Every person has the right to education and participation in intellectual activity.

Article 2

Every African intellectual shall be entitled to the respect of all his or her civil, political, social, economic and cultural rights as stipulated in the International Bill of Rights and the African Charter on Human and People's Rights.

Article 3

No African intellectual shall in any way be persecuted, harassed or intimidated for reasons only of his intellectual work or opinions.

Article 4

Every African intellectual shall enjoy the freedom of movement within his or her country and freedom to travel outside and re-enter the country without let, hindrance or harassment. No administrative or any other action shall directly or indirectly restrict this freedom on account of a person's intellectual opinions, beliefs or activity.

Article 5

Every African intellectual and intellectual community has the right to initiate and develop contacts or establish relations with other intellectuals and intellectual communities provided that they are based on equality and mutual respect.

Article 6

Every African intellectual has the right to pursue intellectual activity, including teaching, research and dissemination of research results, without let or hindrance subject only to universally recognized principles of scientific enquiry and ethical and professional standards.

Article 7

Teaching and researching members of staff and students of institutions of education have the right, directly and through their elected representatives, to initiate participate in and determine academic programmes of their institutions in accordance with the highest standards of education.

Article 8

Teaching and researching members of the intellectual community shall have security of tenure. He or she shall not be dismissed or removed from employment except for reasons of gross misconduct, proven incompetence or negligence incompatible with the academic profession. Disciplinary proceedings for dismissal or removal on grounds stated in this article shall be in accordance with laid down procedures providing for a fair hearing before a democratically elected body of the intellectual community.

Article 9
The intellectual community shall have the rights to express its opinions freely in the media and establish its own media and means of communication.

Section B: Rights to Autonomous Organizations

Article 10
All members of the intellectual community shall have the freedom of association, including the right to form and join trade unions. The right of association includes the right of peaceful assembly and formation of groups, clubs and national and international associations.

Section C: Autonomy of Institutions

Article 11
Institutions of higher education shall be autonomous and independent of the State or any other public authority in conducting their affairs, including administration, and setting up their academic, teaching, research and other related programmes.

Article 12
The autonomy of the Institutions of higher education shall be exercised by democratic means of self-government, involving active participation of all members of the respective academic community.

Chapter II: Obligations of the State

Article 13
The State is obliged to take prompt and appropriate measures in respect of any infringement by state officials of the rights and freedoms of the intellectual community brought to its attention.

Article 14
The State shall not deploy any military, paramilitary, security or intelligence, or any of the like forces within the premises and grounds of institutions of education.

Article 15
The State shall desist from exercising censorship over the works of the intellectual community.

Article 16
The State is obliged to ensure that no official or organ under its control produces or puts into circulation disinformation or rumours calculated to intimidate, bring into disrepute or in any way interfere with the legitimate pursuits of the intellectual community.

Article 17
The State shall continuously ensure adequate funding for research institutions and higher education.

Article 18
The State shall desist from pre venting or imposing conditions on the movement or employment of African intellectuals from other countries in its country.
Chapter III: Social Responsibility

Article 19
Members of the intellectual community are obliged to discharge their roles and functions with competence, integrity and to the best of their abilities. They should perform their duties in accordance with ethical and highest scientific standards.

Article 20
Members of the intellectual community have a responsibility to promote the spirit of tolerance towards different views and positions and enhance democratic debate and discussion.

Article 21
No one group of the intellectual community shall indulge in harassment, domination or oppressive behaviour towards another group. All differences among the intellectual community shall be approached and resolved in the spirit of equality, non-discrimination and democracy.

Article 22
The intellectual community has the responsibility to struggle for and participate in the struggle of the popular forces for their rights and emancipation.

Article 23
No member of the intellectual community shall participate in or be a party to any endeavour which may work to the detriment of the people or the intellectual community or compromise scientific, ethical and professional principles and standards.

Article 24
The intellectual community is obliged to show solidarity and give sanctuary to any member who is persecuted for his intellectual activity.

Article 25
The intellectual community is obliged to encourage and contribute to affirmative actions, to redress historical and contemporary inequalities based on gender, nationality or any other social disadvantage.

Article 26

Members of the intellectual community may further elaborate and concretize the norms and standards set herein at regional and pan-African level.

Article 27

It is incumbent on the African intellectual community to form its own organizations to monitor and publicize violations of the rights and freedoms stipulated herein.

Name of Representative	Name of Association	Name of Institution	Signature
Mr Eligius Benjamin Danda	MUCASA (Moshi University College Academic Staff Association)	Moshi University of Cooperative and Business Studies, Tanzania	signed]
Dr Elifuraha G. Mtalo	ARISA (UCLAS Academic Academic Staff Assembly)	University College of Lands and Architectural (UCLAS), Tanzania	[signed]
Mr Salim Othman Hamad	SUZAASA (The State University of Zanzibar Academic Staff Association)	The State University of Zanzibar (SUZA), Tanzania	[signed]
Prof. Chachage S. L. Chachage	UDASA (University of Dar es Salaam Academic Staff Assembly)	University of Dar es Salaam, Tanzania	[signed]
Prof John H. Nderutu	UASU (University Academic Staff Union)	University of Nairobi, Kenya	[signed]
Mr Musaha Esebe	UASU (University Academic Staff Union)	Moi University, Kenya	[signed]
Mr Muga K'olale	UASU (University Academic Staff Union)	Egerton University, Kenya	[signed]
Dr Ezra Mishambi Twesigomwe	MUASA (Makerere University Staff Association)	Makerere University, Uganda	[signed]
Mr Lubowa Luwalira	Zanzibar University Staff Academic Assembly	Zanzibar University, Zanzibar	[signed]
Prof. D. M. Kambarage	SUASA (Sokoine University Academic Staff Assembly)	Sokoine University of Agriculture, Tanzania	[signed]

The Dar-es-Salaam Declaration on Academic Freedom and Social Responsibility of Academics

Preamble

We are living in momentous times, ridden with crises but full of hope.

The stringent conditions of the international Shylocks have begun to put a squeeze on education in a dramatic fashion. Tanzania, like the rest of the African continent, finds itself entangled in a web of socio-economic crises. As budgetary allocations for education become minuscule, education is threatening to become the preserve of a minority of the wealthy and influential in our society.

The state has become increasingly authoritarian. Authoritarianism is being further reinforced as the crisis-ridden government fails to offer palpable solutions. Witness the increasingly greater, deeper, and more frequent encroachments on academic freedom and freedom to pursue truth and knowledge, particularly at the universities and other institutions of higher education.

These are times of crises. But they are also times of hope. As People's free and independent existence is in question, they are beginning to question the existence of unfree and right-less polities.

We, as academics, intellectuals, and purveyors of knowledge have a human obligation and a social responsibility towards our People's Struggle for Rights, Freedom, Social Transformation and Human Emancipation. Our participation in the struggle of our people is inseparably linked with the struggle forthe autonomy of institutions of higher education and the freedom to pursue knowledge without let, hindrance, and interference from persons in authority.

In 1984, for the first time since independence, the Constitution of the United Republic of Tanzania was amended to include a Bill of Rights. The

Constitution provides for the right to education and the right toopinion and expression which include academic freedom.

Tanzania subscribes to the United Nations' Universal Declaration of Human Rights, has ratified the International Covenants (1966) and the UNESCO Convention against Discrimination in Education, and is a Party to the African Charter on Human and Peoples' Rights. These instruments unambiguously declare for the right of education and freedom of opinion, expression, and dissemination of information.

But rights are not simply given; they are won. And even when won, they cannot endure unless protected, nurtured, and continuously defended against encroachment and curtailment.

NOW THEREFORE, WE the delegates of the Staff Associations of Institutions of Higher Education in Tanzania, meeting in Dar es Salaam, this 19th day of April, 1990 do Solemnly Adopt and Proclaim this Declaration.

PART I

BASIC PRINCIPLES

Chapter One: Education for Human Emancipation

1. Every human being has the right to wholesome education. Education shall be directed to the full development of human personality.
2. Access to education shall be equal and equitable.
3. Education *shall prepare a person to strive for and to participate fully in the emancipation of the* human being and society from oppression, domination, and subjugation.
4. Education shall enable a person to overcome prejudices related to gender, race, nation, ethnicity, religion, class, culture, and such like. Education shall inculcate in every person respect for all human culture developed by humankind.
5. Education shall develop critical faculties, inculcate the spirit of scientific enquiry, and encourage the pursuit of knowledge and the search for the whole truth in the interest of social transformation and human liberation.
6. Education shall be secular. Religious instruction shall be separate from secular education and imparted to those wanting to partake of it voluntarily.
7. Education shall make every person conscious of ecology and the need to protect the environment.

Chapter Two: Obligations of the State

8. The State should guarantee to every resident equal, equitable, and wholesome education without discrimination of any kind as to race, colour,

gender, language, religion, political or other opinion, national or social origin, economic condition, physical or mental disability, birth or other status.

9. The State should make available an adequate proportion of the national income to ensure in practice the full realization of the right to education. The State shall bind itself constitutionally to provide a nationally agreed minimum proportion of the national income for education.

10. The State should take affirmative action where necessary to redress historical and contemporary inequalities in access to education based on national, racial, social, or gender differences or arising from physical disabilities.

Chapter Three: Rights and Obligations of Communities

11. In the exercise of the right to self-determination, nationalities, communities, and like collectivities shall have the right to provide education. Such education shall be in conformity with the Basic Principles and other provisions of this Declaration.

12. It will be part of the obligation of a non-governmental organization involved in the provision of education to contribute towards affirmative actions in conformity with the spirit of article 10.

13. It will be part of the obligation of a community or a nationality to struggle against prejudices, attitudes, and beliefs which in any form or manner prevent or discourage its members from partaking of education on an equal basis.

PART II ACADEMIC FREEDOM

Chapter One: Rights and Freedoms

14. All members of the academic community have the right to fulfil their functions of teaching, doing research, writing, learning, exchanging and disseminating information, and providing services without fear of interference or repression from the State or any other public authority.

15. Civil, political, social, economic and cultural rights of members of the academic community recognized by the United Nations Covenants on Human Rights shall be respected. In particular, all members of the academic community shall enjoy freedom of thought, enquiry, conscience, expression, assembly, and association as well as the right to liberty, security, and integrity of the person

16. All members of the academic community shall enjoy freedom of movement within the country and freedom to travel outside and re-enter the country without let, hindrance, or harassment. This freedom may be

restricted only on grounds of public health, morality, or in circumstances of clear, present, and imminent danger to the nation and its independence....

17. Access to the academic community shall be equal for all members of society without hindrance. On the basis of ability, every resident has the right, without discrimination of any kind, to become part of the academic community as a student, researcher, teacher, worker, or administrator without prejudice to any necessary affirmative action in that behalf.

18. Teaching and researching members of staff and students, directly and through their democratically elected representatives, shall have the right to initiate, participate in, and determine academic programmes of their institutions in accordance with the highest standards of education and the Basic Principles.

19. All members of the academic community with research functions have the right to carry out; research without interference, subject to the universal principles and methods of scientific enquiry. In particular, researchers shall not be denied information or permission to do, or hindered in any way from doing, research on any ground except for reasons of public health and morality, or, in circumstances of clear, present, and imminent danger to the nation and its independence....

20. All members of the academic community with teaching functions have the right to teach without any interference, subject to the generally accepted principles, standards, and methods of teaching.

21. A member of the academic community shall have the right to demand and receive explanation from any organ, official, or administrator of the institution on its/her/his performance affecting her/him or the academic community at large.

22. Save where it is contrary to morality or principles of democracy, all members of the academic community shall enjoy the freedom to maintain contact with their counterparts in any part of the world as well as the freedom to pursue the development of their educational capacities.

23. All students shall enjoy freedom of study, including the right to choose the field of study from available courses and the right to receive official recognition of this knowledge and experience acquired. Institutions of higher education shall aim to satisfy the professional and educational needs and aspirations of [their] students.

24. All institutions of higher education shall guarantee the participation of students in their governing bodies. They shall respect the right of students, individually or collectively, to express and disseminate opinions on any national or international question.

25. It Is the right of students on reasonable grounds to challenge or differ with their instructors in academic matters without fear of reprisal or victimization or [of] being subjected to any other form of direct or indirect prejudice.

Chapter Two: Autonomous Academic Organizations

26. All members of the academic community shall have freedom of association, including the right to form and to join independent and autonomous trade unions. The right of association includes the right of peaceful assembly and formation of groups, clubs, associations, and such other bodies to further the academic and professional interests of the members of the academic community.

27. All members of the academic community shall have the right to write, print, and publish their own newspapers or any other form of media including wall literature, posters, and pamphlets. The exercise of this right shall have due regard to the obligation of the members of the academic community not to interfere with the right of others to privacy and in any manner or form to unreasonably arouse religious, ethnic, national, or gender hatred.

Chapter Three: Security of Tenure

28. All members of the academic community shall be entitled to a fair and reasonable remuneration commensurate with their social and academic responsibilities so that they may discharge their roles with human dignity, integrity, and independence.

29. Teaching and researching members of the academic community, once confirmed in employment, shall have security of tenure. No teaching member or researcher shall be dismissed or removed from employment except for reasons of gross misconduct or proven incompetence or negligence incompatible with the academic profession. Disciplinary proceedings for dismissal or removal on grounds stated in this article shall be in accordance with laid down procedures providing for a fair hearing before a democratically elected body of the academic community.

30. No teaching or researching member of the academic community shall be transferred to another post or position within or outside the institution without her/his prior consent.

31. A member of the academic community has the right to know any report, adverse or otherwise, on her/his performance made or received by relevant officials or organs of the institution in the course of the execution of their duties.

Chapter Four: Obligations of the State and Administration

32. The State and any other public authority shall respect the rights and freedoms of the academic community enshrined in this Declaration. The State is obliged to take prompt and appropriate measures in respect of any infringement by State officials of the rights and freedoms of the academic community brought to its attention.

33. Subject to article 40, the State shall not deploy any military, paramilitary, security or intelligence, or any other like forces within the premises and grounds of... institutions of higher education.

34. The State is obliged to ensure that no official or organ under its control produces or puts into circulation disinformation or rumors calculated to intimidate, bring into disrepute, or in any way interfere with the legitimate pursuits of the academic community.

35. The State and the administration are obliged to ensure that the terms and conditions of service of the academic community are not, directly or indirectly, changed adversely or eroded such that the exercise of the rights and freedoms of the academic community is effectively undermined.

36. The State or the administration shall not impose direct or indirect conditions, procedures, or any other form of restrictions which in effect nullify or curtail the rights and freedoms enshrined in this Declaration.

37. The administration is under an obligation not to divulge any information regarding members of the academic community which may be used to their detriment in any criminal or other investigation or proceedings of [similar] nature.

PART III AUTONOMY OF INSTITUTIONS OF HIGHER EDUCATION

38. Institutions of higher education shall be independent of the State or any other public authority in conducting their affairs and setting up their academic, teaching, research, and other related programmes. The State is under an obligation not to interfere with the autonomy of institutions of higher education.

39. The autonomy of the institutions of higher education shall be exercised by democratic means of self-government, involving active participation of all members of the respective academic communities. All members of the academic community shall have the right and opportunity, without discrimination of any kind, to take part in the conduct of academic and administrative affairs. All governing bodies of institutions of higher education shall be freely elected. They shall [consist] of, among others, members of different sectors of the academic community such that the

majority are representatives of students and academic staff. Staff associations shall be represented in these bodies.

40. No armed personnel, military or paramilitary forces, intelligence and security personnel, or forces of law and order shall singly or collectively enter the premises and grounds of institutions of higher education except under the following conditions:

(a) There is clear, present, and imminent danger to life or property of the institution, and such danger cannot be averted without the intervention of the forces of the State; and

(b) The Head of the institution concerned has invited such intervention in writing; Provided that such invitation shall not be extended without consultation with and approval of a special standing committee of elected representatives of the academic community instituted in that behalf.

PART IV SOCIAL RESPONSIBILITY

Chapter One: Responsibility of Institutions

41. All institutions of higher education shall pursue the fulfillment of economic, social, cultural, civil, and political rights of the people and shall strive to prevent the misuse of science and technology to the detriment of those rights. Institutions of higher education should be critical of conditions of political repression and violations of human rights in our society.

42. All institutions of higher education shall address themselves to the contemporary problems facing our society. To this end, curricula and academic programmes as well as other activities of the institutions shall respond to the needs of the society at large without prejudice to the needs of scientific enquiry and production of knowledge.

43. All institutions of higher education shall extend support to other such institutions and individual members of academic communities, both inside or outside the country, when they are subject to persecution. Such support may be moral or material, and should include refuge and employment or education for victims of persecution.

44. All institutions of higher education should strive to prevent scientific, technological, and other forms of dependence of our society and promote equal partnership of all academic communities of the world in the pursuit and use of knowledge.

45. All institutions of higher education are obliged to offer academic programmes of the highest standard, suitable [for] the professional needs and aspirations of their students.

Chapter Two: Responsibility of Academics

46. All members of the academic community have a responsibility to fulfil their functions and academic roles with competence, integrity, and to the best of their abilities. They should perform their academic functions in accordance with ethical and the highest scientific standards.

47. All members of the academic community shall exercise their rights with responsibility without prejudice to the rights of others and [to] the needs of our society.

48. All members of the academic community have the obligation to inculcate the spirit of tolerance towards differing views and positions and enhance democratic debate and discussion.

49. No member of the academic community shall participate in or be a party to any endeavour which may work to the detriment of the people or the academic community or compromise scientific, ethical, and professional principles and standards.

50. All members of the academic community have a duty to contribute towards redressing historical and contemporary inequalities in our society based on differences of class, beliefs, gender, race, nationality, region and economic condition. Towards this end, all members of the academic community should voluntarily give their time to impart education to disadvantaged sectors of the population.

PART V: RATIFICATION AND ACCESSION

51. This Declaration shall come into force when ratified by the membership of two-thirds of the staff associations of the institutions of higher education attending the inaugural workshop.

52. Any autonomous staff association or autonomous student organization of an institution of higher education in Tanzania may accede to this Declaration by depositing instruments of ratification with the body established in that behalf.

PART VI DEFINITIONS

53. In this Declaration, unless the context otherwise requires,

- "Academic community" covers all those persons teaching, studying, [doing research] or otherwise working at an institution of higher education;

- "Academic freedom" means the freedom of members of the academic community, individually or collectively, in the pursuit, development, and transmission of knowledge, through research, study, discussion, documentation, production, creation, teaching, lecturing, and writing;

- "Administration" means the organs and officials involved in the administration of an institution of higher education.

- "Affirmative action" refers to deliberate action, including positive discrimination, taken as a temporary measure to redress historical or contemporary inequality;

- "Autonomy" means the independence of institutions of higher education and organizations, associations, and groups within these institutions from the State and any other public authority including a political party but not including organizations of civil society; and "autonomous" shall be construed accordingly;

- "Basic Principles" means principles enunciated in Part I of the Declaration, and where the context requires "education" shall be construed to mean education in accordance with the Basic Principles;

- "Community" as used in Chapter Three of Part I herein refers to a national group solidary by virtue of commonality of culture, language, or religious belief and includes neighborhood groups;

- "Independence" in relation to a member of the academic community, the academic community or institution refers to the freedom to pursue the academic profession without compromise;

- "Institution" means an institution of higher education;

- "Institutions of Higher Education" means universities and other post-secondary school institutions offering formal instruction, or conducting research, leading to qualifications of Diplomas or Degree, or like qualifications, but do not include vocational and in-service training centres;

- "Inaugural workshop" means the first meeting of the delegates of the institutions of higher education called to adopt and proclaim this Declaration;

- "Nationality" refers to groups within state societies solidary by virtue of common territory, culture and language.

- "Resident" means any person living in Tanzania including her/his immediate family.

Dar Es Salaam, 19 April 1990

www.ingramcontent.com/pod-product-compliance
Lightning Source LLC
Chambersburg PA
CBHW021822270326
41932CB00007B/304